W9-BJA-647

OTHER BOOKS BY WILLIAM I. KAUFMAN

THE ART OF CREOLE COOKERY

THE ART OF INDIA'S COOKERY

THE NUT COOKBOOK

THE 'I LOVE PEANUT BUTTER' COOKBOOK

THE COFFEE COOKBOOK

THE TEA COOKBOOK

THE CHOCOLATE COOKBOOK

THE HOT DOG COOKBOOK

THE COTTAGE CHEESE COOKBOOK

THE ART OF CASSEROLE COOKERY

THE 'I LOVE GARLIC' COOKBOOK

THE APPLE COOKBOOK

COOKING IN A CASTLE

THE WONDERFUL WORLD OF COOKING (4 Vols.)

THE STANDUP COOKBOOKS (4 Vols.)

THE FISH AND SHELLFISH COOKBOOK

APPETIZERS AND CANAPES

"The
Doubleday

Little Cookbook

Shelf"

APPETIZERS

AND

CANAPES

*

WILLIAM I. KAUFMAN

1968

DOUBLEDAY & COMPANY, INC., GARDEN CITY, N.Y.

LIBRARY OF CONGRESS CATALOG CARD NUMBER 68–22604
COPYRIGHT © 1968 BY WILLIAM I. KAUFMAN
ALL RIGHTS RESERVED
PRINTED IN THE UNITED STATES OF AMERICA
FIRST EDITION

This book is dedicated to my wife, who starts each day with zest and the desire to improve every little "canapé" that life brings.

William I. Kaufman

Contents

Recipes marked with an asterisk (*) may be located by consulting the Index.

Introduction

An appetizer might best be called an appetite-titillation as its sole purpose is to arouse the taste buds of the diner. Appetizers are varied combinations of food flavorings. They are of two types: those which are ideal for service in the living room, den, or on the porch before dinner and which may be offered either as a preamble to a meal or as the first course of the meal itself and those which are only suitable as the first course of a sit-down dinner. Both types of appetizers will be found in this special Little Cookbook.

In serving appetizers most hostesses aim to present something piquant and delicate. They try to include "exotic" or "continental" luxury touches to show their guests how much they care to please. All of these unusual appetizer makings, once so complicated to procure, may be found on the shelves of every modern market. Their presence there permits the hostess to give free rein to her imagination.

The beginning of the meal is a time to set a keynote of good feeling. Nothing adds to that spirit more than attractive food and nothing is more eye-appealing than a well-decorated tray of canapés which have received the unique attention of a cook who cares.

The foundation of the canapé is a small piece of bread

cut into a fancy shape; square, circle, diamond, or oblong. This bread shape may be toasted, fried, or plain. First it should be spread with plain or seasoned butter and then topped with the ingredients that suit the chef's creative taste. Development of modern convenience foods has provided us with a large supply of ready-made toasts and crackers in varying shapes and flavors that are perfect as the base for the up-to-date kind of canapé spreads the reader finds in this volume.

Canapés should be artfully decorated. They look most attractive when they are arranged on large platters surrounded by an assortment of pickles, olives, onions, radishes, and other relishes. Guests should be offered small plates of glass, china, or ceramic which offset the color of the canapés. The use of these small pretty plates permits the guest to help himself to more than one canapé at a time. If a very large crowd is being served however, it is considered perfectly good form in these servantless days to distribute attractive cocktail napkins rather than plates. For even greater ease of service and preparation many canapé spreads can be offered with potato and corn chips, french fries, Fritos, cheese sticks, or pretzels instead of being smoothed over the traditional bread foundation. Served in this manner, they take on an even more delicious texture and taste. Success in achieving novelty in appetizers and canapés depends on the talent, ingenuity, taste, and economic possibilities of each individual culinary artist. Let this small volume, containing as it does a multitude of ideas, lead you to the creation of first course specialties that are particularly "your own," for it is the marriage of tradition with innovation that always produces the most satisfactory results in the art of making appetizers and canapés.

WILLIAM I. KAUFMAN

Appetizers

CHICKEN PATE MOLD

1 tablespoon butter
¼ pound chicken livers
1 small onion, sliced
1 shallot, sliced
1 small apple, pared, cored, and coarsely chopped
¼ teaspoon salt
¼ cup cold water
1 envelope unflavored gelatine

½ cup Chicken Broth,* heated to boiling
Cooked Chicken and Chicken Broth* (remaining ¾ cup broth)
¼ cup mayonnaise
½ cup heavy cream
Truffles

Melt butter in skillet. Add chicken livers, onion, shallot, apple, and salt. Cook slowly 10 minutes over low heat until livers are browned and onion is tender. Put cold water and gelatine in blender container. Cover and process at low to soften gelatine. Add boiling broth. Process until gelatine dissolves. If gelatine granules cling to container, use rubber spatula to scrape sides and push granules into center. When gelatine is dissolved, turn control to high and add liver mixture with chicken and remaining broth, mayonnaise, and cream. Process until smooth. Turn into 4-cup mold. Chill until firm. Unmold and garnish with chopped truffles. *Makes 8 servings*

CHICKEN AND CHICKEN BROTH

1 whole chicken breast	**¼ teaspoon salt**
¾ cup water	**1 chicken bouillon cube**
½ cup sherry	

Simmer all ingredients together in saucepan 30 minutes. Remove meat from bones and cut in pieces. Measure broth and, if necesssary, add water to make 1¼ cups. *Makes 4 cups*

INDIVIDUAL PATE MOLDS

2 envelopes unflavored gelatine	**1 can (5¼ ounces) mousse pâté de foie**
1 can (13 ounces) chicken consommé	**Parsley, minced or gherkins, sliced**

Sprinkle gelatine into ¼ cup consommé. Let stand in saucepan 5 minutes, then place over low heat and cook, stirring constantly, until gelatine dissolves. Combine remaining consommé with gelatine. Put 1½ teaspoons consommé into each ice cube compartment using individual plastic cube forms or plastic ice cube tray to facilitate unmolding without aid of hot water. (A twist of plastic will release mold.) Chill until firm. Cut pâté into 14 pieces. Shape each piece into small ball and put one ball into each compartment. Add enough remaining gelatine to cover ball of pâté completely. Chill until firm. When ready to serve unmold cubes by twisting plastic. Cut each cube in half lengthwise. Serve cut side up. Garnish with minced parsley or thin slices of gherkins. *Makes 28*

YORKSHIRE PUFFS

1 teaspoon salt	4 eggs
1 cup boiling water	1 pound ground beef
½ cup shortening	Shortening for deep-fat frying
1 cup sifted enriched flour	

Combine salt and boiling water in saucepan. Add shortening and bring to a boil. Reduce heat to medium. Add flour all at once, stirring vigorously, until ball forms in center of pan. Cool slightly. Add eggs, one at a time, beating after each addition until mixture is smooth. Mixture should be very stiff. Brown ground beef in skillet. Pour off drippings. Add browned beef to puff mixture. Blend thoroughly. Heat shortening to 365° F. Drop puff mixture by teaspoonfuls into hot shortening. Deep-fat fry 3 to 5 minutes or until golden brown. *Makes 84*

MINIATURE MEATBALLS

1 pound ground beef	Stuffed olives
1 teaspoon salt	Pickled onions
⅛ teaspoon pepper	Barbecue Sauce*

Combine beef, salt, and pepper in mixing bowl. Measure 1 tablespoon seasoned ground beef for each ball. Mold beef around stuffed olive or small pickled onion. Place in shallow baking dish. Bake in 300° F. oven 20 minutes. Serve hot with Barbecue Sauce*. *Makes 40*

BARBECUE SAUCE

2 tablespoons shortening
½ cup chopped onion
2 tablespoons vinegar
2 tablespoons brown sugar
¼ cup lemon juice
1 cup catsup

3 tablespoons Worcestershire sauce
1 cup water
1 teaspoon salt
⅛ teaspoon cayenne

Heat shortening in skillet. Add onion and brown. Pour off drippings. Add remaining ingredients and cook over low heat, stirring frequently, 25 minutes or until thickened. *Makes 2 cups Barbecue Sauce*

NUTTY MEATBALLS

1 pound ground beef
¾ cup finely chopped roasted peanuts
½ teaspoon salt
½ teaspoon onion salt
¼ teaspoon pepper
1 egg, beaten
1 tablespoon soy sauce

¼ cup peanut oil
¼ cup cornstarch
1½ cups water
⅓ cup firmly packed brown sugar
¼ cup vinegar
2 tablespoons soy sauce

Combine ground beef, chopped peanuts, salt, onion salt, and pepper in large mixing bowl. Add beaten egg and 1 tablespoon soy sauce. Mix well. Shape into small meatballs. Heat oil in large skillet and sauté meatballs until tender and cooked through. Remove meatballs from skillet. Drain off excess oil. Combine cornstarch with a small amount of water until smooth. Blend with remaining water. Slowly pour into skillet, stirring constantly, until smooth. Add brown sugar, vinegar, and 2 tablespoons soy sauce. Cook over medium heat, stirring constantly, until mixture thickens and comes to boil. Add meatballs to sauce. Heat through before serving. *Makes about 36*

LAMB PINWHEELS

2 cups ground cooked lamb
½ cup grated American
  cheese
¼ teaspoon rosemary
½ teaspoon salt

⅛ teaspoon pepper
4 drops Tabasco
Biscuit Dough*
½ cup mayonnaise

Combine all ingredients except Biscuit Dough* and mayonnaise in mixing bowl. Blend well. Make Biscuit Dough*. Pat or roll dough into 12×18-inch rectangle. Spread dough with mayonnaise. Top with ground lamb mixture. Roll as for jelly roll starting at longest side. Cut into ½-inch slices. Place on ungreased baking sheet and bake in 425° F. oven 12 to 15 minutes. *Makes 36*

BISCUIT DOUGH

2 cups sifted enriched flour   4 to 6 tablespoons shortening
1 tablespoon baking powder   ⅓ to ½ cup milk
¾ teaspoon salt

Sift together flour, baking powder, and salt into mixing bowl.
Cut in shortening until mixture forms fine even crumb. Add
milk to make a soft dough. Turn onto a lightly floured surface
and knead gently ½ minute.

LAMB RING AROUNDS

2 cups ground cooked lamb   ¼ teaspoon dillweed
½ cup grated American   ½ teaspoon salt
    cheese   ⅛ teaspoon pepper
½ cup mayonnaise   Biscuit Dough*

Combine all ingredients except Biscuit Dough* in mixing bowl.
Blend well. Make Biscuit Dough*. Pat or roll out ⅛ inch
thickness. With 2-inch biscuit cutter cut into 32 thin rounds.
Spread half the rounds with ground lamb mixture. With 1-inch
biscuit cutter cut holes from remaining rounds and place
doughnut-shaped piece on each lamb-topped round. Place on
ungreased baking sheet. Bake in 425° F. oven 12 to 15
minutes. *Makes 16*

GROUND LAMB KEBABS

1 **pound ground shoulder of lamb**	¼ **teaspoon ground black pepper**
2 **tablespoons instant minced onion**	1 **tablespoon parsley flakes**
¾ **teaspoon ground coriander**	1 **large egg**
1 **teaspoon salt**	1 **tablespoon cooking oil**
¼ **teaspoon instant garlic powder**	

Combine all ingredients in mixing bowl. Shape into 1-inch balls. Cover and refrigerate 3 hours to blend seasonings. String on skewers and broil in 350° F. oven or over charcoal 10 to 15 minutes or until tender and cooked through. Serve hot. *Makes 20*

ORIENTAL LAMB BALLS

2 **pounds ground lamb**	½ **teaspoon ginger**
½ **cup fine bread crumbs**	⅛ **teaspoon salt**
½ **cup finely chopped almonds or pecans**	¼ **cup cornstarch**
3 **tablespoons soy sauce**	3 **tablespoons shortening**
	Oriental Sauce*

Combine all ingredients except cornstarch, shortening, and Oriental Sauce* in mixing bowl. Blend well. Form mixture into

balls about 1 inch in diameter. Roll in cornstarch. Heat shortening in skillet and brown lamb balls. While lamb is cooking
make Oriental Sauce*. Pour drippings from skillet and add hot
Oriental Sauce* to lamb balls. *Makes 6 dozen*

ORIENTAL SAUCE

1 tablespoon cornstarch	½ cup soy sauce
1 teaspoon ginger	½ cup tarragon vinegar
½ cup brown sugar	1 cup pineapple juice

Mix cornstarch, ginger, and brown sugar in saucepan. Gradu-
ally stir in soy sauce, vinegar, and pineapple juice. Bring to boil
and cook over low heat until thick and glossy. *Makes 2 cups
sauce*

HAM SALAD PUFFS

1 teaspoon salt	1 cup sifted enriched flour
1 cup boiling water	4 eggs
½ cup shortening	Ham Salad Filling*

Combine salt and boiling water in saucepan. Add shortening
and bring to a boil. Reduce heat to medium and add flour all
at once, stirring vigorously until ball forms in center of pan.
Cool slightly. Add eggs, one at a time, beating after each
addition until mixture is smooth. Mixture should be very stiff.
Allowing 1 teaspoon of mixture for each puff, drop batter on

greased cooky sheets and bake in 400° F. oven 15 to 18 minutes. Cool. Cut tops from puffs. Fill each puff with Ham Salad Filling*. Replace tops. *Makes 84*

HAM SALAD FILLING

4 cups ground cooked ham	¼ cup dairy sour cream
1 cup grated Cheddar cheese	1 teaspoon dry mustard
1 cup mayonnaise	½ cup pickle relish

Combine all ingredients in mixing bowl. Blend well. Use to fill puffs. *Makes 6½ cups*

HAM-STUFFED CELERY

1 cup ground cooked ham	¼ teaspoon salt
½ cup grated carrot	⅛ teaspoon pepper
½ cup salad dressing	6 ribs celery, each 8 inches
1½ teaspoons prepared	long
horseradish	

Mix all ingredients except celery stalks in mixing bowl. Blend thoroughly. Wash celery, cut into 2-inch pieces, and fill with 1 tablespoon ham-carrot mixture. *Makes 24*

HAM, CHEESE, AND PICKLE ROUNDS

2 cups ground cooked ham   ½ teaspoon dry mustard
½ cup grated Cheddar cheese   ¼ cup pickle relish
½ cup mayonnaise   Unsliced sandwich bread
2 tablespoons dairy sour   Sweet pickles
  cream

Combine all ingredients except bread and sweet pickles in mixing bowl. Blend well. Cut unsliced bread along the length into ½-inch-thick slices. Remove crusts. Roll bread to ⅛ inch thickness with rolling pin. Spread each rolled slice of bread with ½ cup ham filling. Place five sweet pickles on end of bread. Roll, as a jelly roll, starting with pickle-lined end of bread. Wrap rolls in protective wrap. Chill thoroughly. Before serving, cut into ¼-inch-thick rounds.   *Makes 64*

HAM-STUFFED EGGS

1 cup ground cooked ham   2 tablespoons mayonnaise
½ teaspoon salt   6 hard-cooked eggs
⅛ teaspoon pepper   Additional ground cooked
1 teaspoon prepared mustard   ham for garnish
2 tablespoons vinegar   Parsley

Combine first 6 ingredients in mixing bowl. Cut eggs in half lengthwise. Separate yolks from whites. Set whites aside. Mash yolks and add to ham mixture. Fill egg whites with mixture, using fork or pastry tube. Garnish with additional ground cooked ham and parsley. *Makes 12*

SWEDISH PORK APPETIZERS

4 pounds boned pork loin, or shoulder cut in 1-inch cubes
½ cup light molasses
½ cup catsup
½ cup chopped onion
1 clove garlic, minced
4 narrow strips orange peel, diced

Juice ½ orange
¼ cup vinegar
½ teaspoon prepared mustard
¼ teaspoon salt
½ teaspoon Worcestershire sauce
¼ teaspoon Tabasco

Place pork cubes in shallow baking pan and bake in a 300° F. oven 45 minutes. Meanwhile, combine remaining ingredients in saucepan and simmer 5 minutes. Drain fat from pork and pour hot sauce over meat. Roast 1 hour more, basting occasionally. *Makes 12 to 16 servings*

LIVER SAUSAGE APPETIZERS

1 pound liver sausage
Chopped salted peanuts
Stuffed green olives or pickled onions

Chopped parsley
Pretzel sticks

Allowing about 2 teaspoonfuls for each ball, shape half of liver sausage into 20 balls. Roll in chopped salted peanuts.

Shape remaining half of liver sausage around 20 stuffed olives or pickled onions according to preference. Roll in parsley. Insert pretzel stick into each liver sausage ball. *Makes 40*

SALAMI TREATS

1 package (3 ounces) cream
    cheese, softened
1 tablespoon dairy sour
    cream
1 teaspoon prepared
    horseradish
½ teaspoon chopped parsley
1 tablespoon grated onion
12 slices salami

Combine cream cheese, sour cream, horseradish, parsley, and onion in mixing bowl. Blend well. Spread 5 slices of salami with half the cream cheese mixture, stacking them to form cylinder. Top with 6th slice of salami. Repeat for second cylinder. Wrap each cylinder in protective wrap. Chill. Just before serving cut each cylinder into 6 wedges. *Makes 12*

SALAMI APPLE WEDGES

3 tablespoons cream cheese,
    softened
1 teaspoon lemon juice
½ teaspoon grated lemon
    rind
1 large tart apple, cored
6 slices salami

Combine cream cheese, lemon juice, and lemon rind in mixing bowl. Cut apple into rings, ¼ inch thick. Spread cream cheese mixture on apple rings. Place 1 apple ring between 2 salami slices. Repeat for each sandwich. Wrap in protective wrap. Chill. Just before serving cut each sandwich into 6 wedges. *Makes 18*

BACON SALAMI BALLS

1 package (½ pound) bacon
8 ounces processed American cheese
1 package hard salami

3 tablespoons milk
2 teaspoons Worcestershire sauce

Cook bacon until crisp. Drain and crumble. Reserve. Grind cheese and salami together in mixing bowl. Add milk and Worcestershire sauce and mix well. Shape into tiny balls (about 1 teaspoonful in each) and roll in crumbled bacon. Chill before serving. Serve on food picks. *Makes 35 to 40*

BACON CHEESE LOGS

1 package (1 pound) bacon
1 package (8 ounces) cream cheese, softened
½ cup chopped pecans
¼ teaspoon garlic salt

¼ teaspoon Worcestershire sauce
4 drops Tabasco
1 tablespoon chili powder
Crackers

Cook bacon until crisp. Drain and crumble into mixing bowl. Blend with all remaining ingredients except chili powder and crackers. Shape into 2 rolls about 1 inch in diameter. Sprinkle chili powder on waxed paper. Roll logs in chili powder to coat evenly. Wrap tightly in waxed paper. Chill. Slice and serve on crackers. *Makes 60*

SHRIMP DILL MOLD

½ cup cold tomato juice
2 envelopes unflavored
    gelatine
1 cup boiling tomato juice
½ teaspoon salt
¼ cup chili sauce
2 tablespoons lemon juice
1 teaspoon Worcestershire
    sauce
¼ teaspoon Tabasco

1 tablespoon dried dillweed
1 tablespoon prepared
    horseradish
½ cup dry white wine
1 pint dairy sour cream
¾ pound cooked cleaned
    shrimp
Additional shrimp and dill
    for garnish

Put cold tomato juice and gelatine in blender container. Cover and process on low to soften gelatine. Add boiling tomato juice. Process until gelatine dissolves. If gelatine granules cling to side of container, use rubber spatula to scrape sides and push granules into center. When gelatine is dissolved, turn control to high and add all remaining ingredients except shrimp. Process until smooth. Stop blender. Add shrimp. Chop shrimp by turning to high and off quickly several times. Turn entire mixture into 5-cup mold and chill until firm. Unmold and garnish with additional shrimp and dill. *Makes 10 servings (5 cups)*

SHRIMP ACAPULCO

½ cup minced onion
½ cup pickle relish
½ cup minced parsley
2 tablespoons minced chives
2 tablespoons capers
¼ cup olive oil
½ teaspoon salt
½ teaspoon coarsely ground
   black pepper

⅓ cup wine vinegar
1 teaspoon sugar
4 cups water
2 pounds fresh or frozen
   shrimp, cleaned, deveined
Lettuce, watercress, or
   parsley

Combine onion, relish, parsley, chives, capers, olive oil, salt, pepper, vinegar, and sugar in flat bowl with cover. Set aside. Bring water to boil in deep kettle. Add shrimp and cook one to 4 minutes, depending on size of shrimp, until just pink. Discard 2 cups of cooking stock. Add remainder of stock to pickling mixture. Add shrimp. Cover and let cool 1 hour at room temperature, stirring occasionally. Place in refrigerator and chill 24 hours. Drain shrimp and serve on food picks or on bed of crisp greens. *Makes about 36*

LEMON-DILL FRIED SHRIMP

2 tablespoons salad oil
2 tablespoons butter or
   margarine
2 pounds raw shrimp,
   cleaned, deveined
½ teaspoon salt

Coarsely ground black
   pepper
1 teaspoon dried dillweed
3 tablespoons fresh lemon
   juice

Heat oil and butter in large skillet. Add shrimp. Sprinkle with salt, pepper, and dill. Fry 1 minute on each side or until shrimp turn pink. Pour lemon juice over shrimp. Cover skillet and steam 4 to 5 minutes more. Serve hot or cold. *Makes 10 to 12 servings*

SHRIMP-DILL APPETIZER MOLDS

2 envelopes unflavored
   gelatine
1½ cups tomato juice
2 tablespoons lemon juice
¼ cup chili sauce
1 teaspoon Worcestershire
   sauce
¼ teaspoon Tabasco

1 tablespoon dried dillweed
1 pint dairy sour cream
2 cups (¾ pound) finely
   chopped cooked and
   shelled shrimp
Additional shrimp and dill
   sprigs for garnish, if
   desired

Sprinkle gelatine over tomato juice in saucepan. Place over moderate heat and stir constantly 2 to 3 minutes or until gelatine is dissolved. Remove from heat. Stir in lemon juice, chili sauce, Worcestershire sauce, Tabasco, and dill. When mixture is cool, stir in sour cream. Beat until smooth. Stir in shrimp. Turn into individual molds or 5-cup mold. Chill until firm. Unmold. Garnish with whole shrimp and sprigs of dill, if desired. *Makes 10 to 12 servings*

SHRIMP APPETIZER

2 tablespoons butter or margarine	**1 teaspoon minced onion**
1 tablespoon flour	**1 can (6 ounces) shrimp**
1 can (4 ounces) mushroom pieces, drained, liquid reserved	**1 tablespoon chopped parsley**
	4 tablespoons minced green pepper
½ teaspoon Tabasco, divided	**1 hard-cooked egg, chopped**
¼ teaspoon salt	**1 package pastry mix**
	1 egg, beaten

Melt butter in saucepan. Add flour and stir until smooth. Dice mushrooms finely. Add reserved mushroom liquid to flour mixture with ¼ teaspoon Tabasco, salt, and onion. Cook, stirring constantly, until mixture thickens and comes to a boil. Cool. Wash and drain shrimp. Dice finely. Add to sauce with mushrooms, parsley, green pepper, and egg. Mix well. Prepare pastry according to package directions, using remaining ¼ teaspoon Tabasco with water. Divide in half. On waxed paper, roll each half into a 12-inch square. Spread with filling. Cut each square in half lengthwise. Roll all four oblongs as for jelly roll. Cut each roll into 6 pieces. Place on baking sheet. Brush rolls lightly with beaten egg. Bake in a 425° F. oven 20 to 25 minutes, or until browned. *Makes 24*

SHRIMP SAUSAGE APPETIZERS

1 pound Italian link sausage, cut in slices	2 tablespoons paprika
2 medium onions, sliced	2 teaspoons salt
2 pounds shrimp, shelled and deveined	½ teaspoon basil leaves
1 cup beer or ale	1 tablespoon cornstarch
	Water

Sauté sausage and onion in large skillet until golden on all sides. Drain until only about 2 tablespoons fat remain in pan. Add shrimp. Sauté only until shrimp becomes pink. Add beer, paprika, salt, and basil leaves. Cover and simmer 5 minutes. Combine cornstarch and a little water. Push shrimp and sausage mixture to one side of pan. Blend cornstarch into beer, stirring constantly, until smooth and clear. Turn sauce, shrimp, and sausage into chafing dish. Serve shrimp and sausage with food picks. *Makes 12 servings*

SHERRIED AVOCADO-CRAB MEAT APPETIZER

½ cup catsup	Dash cayenne
¼ cup mayonnaise	1 can (6½ ounces) crab meat
¼ cup sherry	1 cup diced avocado
1 teaspoon lemon juice	½ cup finely diced celery

Combine catsup, mayonnaise, wine, lemon juice, and cayenne in mixing bowl. Beat until well blended. Chill 1 hour or more. Shortly before serving mix sauce with other ingredients, tossing lightly to combine. *Makes 6 servings*

VARIATION

Lobster, shrimp, or tuna may be substituted for crab meat.

ESCOVITCHE FISH

1 pound fish fillets
3 tablespoons butter or
  margarine
1 cup cider vinegar
1 tablespoon green pepper
  flakes
4 teaspoons instant minced
  onion

½ teaspoon whole allspice
1½ teaspoons salt
⅛ teaspoon garlic powder
1 hot red pepper, 1½ inches
  long (broken in half)

Rinse fish and cut into 1½-inch squares. Heat butter in skillet and fry fish slowly over low heat. Place fish in flat casserole. Combine remaining ingredients in small saucepan. Bring to boil and cook 1 minute. Pour sauce over fish. Marinate at least 24 hours before serving, turning fish from time to time. *Makes 42 to 48*

SEAFOOD COOLERS

1 package (12 ounces)
  frozen halibut steaks
Boiling water
1 teaspoon grated onion
½ cucumber, washed and
  peeled
¼ cup salad dressing or
  mayonnaise

1 tablespoon lemon juice
½ teaspoon salt
¼ teaspoon pepper
¼ cup dairy sour cream
Buttered pumpernickel
  rounds
Stuffed olives or parsley
  sprigs

Thaw halibut steaks enough to separate. Place in boiling water. Bring water to simmer, cover and cook 10 to 15 minutes or until fish flakes easily. Remove from cooking liquid and cool enough to handle. Remove skin and center bone. Flake fish into mixing bowl. Add onion. Grate the outside white part of cucumber, avoiding center seed portion. Squeeze to drain liquid. Add to flaked halibut. Combine salad dressing, lemon juice, salt, and pepper. Fold into fish. Add as much sour cream as necessary to permit mixture to mound. Taste and correct seasoning if desired. Spread mixture on bread rounds. Garnish with slice of olive or parsley sprig. *Makes about 2 cups*

AFRICAN APPETIZER

1 package (9 ounces) frozen lobster tails (about 3 small tails)	**¼ teaspoon curry powder**
	¼ teaspoon Tabasco
	¼ teaspoon salt
½ cup mayonnaise	**¼ cup chopped celery**
1 tablespoon milk	**1 banana**
2 teaspoons lemon juice	**Lettuce**

Cook lobster according to package directions. Let cool. Remove meat from shell. Chop and chill. When lobster is thoroughly chilled, combine mayonnaise, milk, and lemon juice in mixing bowl. Add curry powder, Tabasco, and salt. Toss with lobster and celery. Just before serving, slice banana and gently stir into lobster curry. Serve on lettuce. *Makes 4 servings*

CURRIED SHRIMP

2 packages (8 ounces each) frozen uncooked shrimp, cleaned, deveined
2½ tablespoons butter or margarine
½ teaspoon curry powder

Let shrimp thaw. Preheat broiler. Melt butter in saucepan over low heat. Add curry powder and stir to blend. (Do not let butter burn.) Arrange shrimp on foil or pie pan. Brush with curried butter and broil 7 minutes on one side. Turn, brush again with curried butter, and broil 7 minutes on other side until shrimp is golden brown, basting once or twice more with curried butter during broiling. Serve hot. *Makes 30*

ANGELS ON HORSEBACK

1 pint small oysters
12 thin slices of bacon

Drain oysters. Cut bacon slices in half and wrap each half slice of bacon around an oyster. Secure with toothpicks. Place in shallow baking dish or on broiler rack. Bake in 450° F. oven 10 to 15 minutes until bacon is crisp or broil 4 inches from the source of heat 7 minutes until bacon is crisp, turning once. *Makes 24*

OYSTER-STUFFED MUSHROOM CAPS

12 small oysters   **⅛ teaspoon salt**
2 tablespoons butter   **12 large mushroom caps**
2 tablespoons sherry or
lemon juice

Drain oysters. Melt butter in saucepan. Stir in sherry or lemon juice, and salt. Dip oysters in hot butter sauce and place one in each mushroom cap. Arrange caps in shallow, greased baking dish. Pour remaining sauce over. Bake in a 400° F. oven 10 to 12 minutes or boil 4 inches from the source of heat 3 to 4 minutes. *Makes 12*

BUNUELOS DE SALMON

¼ cup butter or margarine	¼ teaspoon salt
½ cup boiling water	2 large eggs
½ cup sifted all-purpose flour	Salmon Filling*

Add butter to boiling water in saucepan over high heat. When butter is melted add flour and salt all at once and cook 2 to 3 minutes, stirring vigorously with a spoon until mixture leaves the sides of pan in smooth, compact mass and until a metal spoon pressed into mixture leaves a clear impression. Remove mixture from heat. Add eggs, one at a time, beating until each is blended and mixture is smooth. Continue beating until mixture forms stiff dough. Drop by heaping half-teaspoonfuls onto greased cooky sheets, 1 inch apart. Bake in 450° F. oven 10 minutes. Reduce heat to 350° F. and bake 10 minutes more. Cool and fill with Salmon Filling*. *Makes 48*

SALMON FILLING

⅓ cup sweet pepper flakes
3 tablespoons water
½ jar (4 ounces) pimiento, finely chopped
2 cans (7½ ounces each) red salmon
1 tablespoon butter or margarine

2 tablespoons flour
½ cup milk
1½ teaspoons salt
1½ teaspoons marjoram leaves
½ teaspoon ground black pepper
⅛ teaspoon garlic powder

Soften sweet pepper flakes in water in mixing bowl. Add pimiento and salmon. Set aside. Melt butter or margarine in large saucepan over medium heat. Blend in flour stirring until smooth. Remove saucepan from heat. Add milk. Return to heat and cook 2 or 3 minutes, stirring constantly, until mixture is very thick. Remove from heat and stir in seasonings and salmon mixture. Return to heat. Bring to boil and cook 5 minutes more, stirring constantly until heated through.

TUNA MOUSSE

1 envelope unflavored gelatine
2 tablespoons lemon juice
2 tablespoons cold water
⅓ cup boiling water
¾ cup mayonnaise
1 teaspoon dried dillweed
¼ teaspoon paprika
½ teaspoon Tabasco

2 cans (6½ or 7 ounces each) tuna in vegetable oil, drained
¾ cup heavy cream
1 small onion, quartered
Ripe olives
Pimiento-stuffed olives

Sprinkle gelatine over lemon juice and cold water in blender container. Allow to stand while assembling other ingredients. Add boiling water. Cover and process at low speed until gelatine dissolves. Add mayonnaise, dillweed, paprika, Tabasco, tuna, heavy cream, and onion. Process at high speed until onion is chopped. Turn into 4-cup mold. Chill. Unmold on platter and garnish with olives. *Makes 16 to 24 servings*

TUNA BITES

1 can (6½ or 7 ounces)
  tuna, drained
1 cup French dressing
3 medium-sized sweet
  gherkins, sliced in ½-inch
  slices

Break tuna into pieces in mixing bowl. Pour French dressing over tuna and chill 1 hour. To serve, place 1 gherkin slice and 1 tuna chunk on each food pick. *Makes 12*

SARDINE APPETIZER

¾ cup catsup
1 tablespoon prepared
  horseradish
6 drops Tabasco
2 tablespoons lemon juice

¼ teaspoon salt
⅛ teaspoon pepper
2 cans (3¼ ounces each)
  sardines, drained
Cocktail sauce

Combine all ingredients except sardines and cocktail sauce in mixing bowl. Blend well. Let stand 2 hours at room temperature to blend flavors. Chill until ready to use. For each serving, place 2 or 3 sardines on a lettuce leaf. Serve with chilled cocktail sauce. *Makes 4 to 6 servings*

MAINE SARDINE DEVILED EGGS

6 hard-cooked eggs	¼ teaspoon curry powder
1 can (3¼ ounces) sardines, mashed, drained	¼ teaspoon salt
4 tablespoons mayonnaise	⅛ teaspoon pepper
¼ teaspoon dry mustard	Paprika

Cut eggs in half lengthwise. Remove yolks to mixing bowl and mash. Add sardines, mayonnaise, dry mustard, curry powder, salt, and pepper and blend well. Fill egg whites with sardine-egg yolk mixture. Top with dash of paprika. *Makes 12*

MARINATED SARDINES

1 clove garlic	1 teaspoon salt
2 cans (3¼ ounces each) sardines, drained	⅛ teaspoon ground black pepper
1 cup very thinly sliced cucumbers	2 tablespoons white wine
¼ cup very thinly sliced onion	2 tablespoons lemon juice
	1 cup dairy sour cream

Rub shallow dish with cut clove garlic. Arrange sardines in bottom of dish. Cover with cucumber. Top cucumber with onion. Combine salt, pepper, wine, lemon juice, and sour cream in mixing bowl. Blend well. Pour over sardines. Cover and let stand at room temperature 2 hours to blend flavors. Chill at least 1 hour before serving. *Makes 4 to 5 servings*

SARDINE-STUFFED ONIONS

6 medium-sized onions	2 eggs, divided
Salted boiling water	1 teaspoon salt
3 cans (3¼ ounces each)	⅛ teaspoon pepper
sardines, drained	4 tablespoons flour
2 tablespoons pickle relish	½ cup dry bread crumbs
1 tablespoon melted butter	Shortening
or margarine	

Peel onions. Place in saucepan and cook in rapidly boiling salted water to cover 30 minutes, or until tender. Drain onions and remove centers, leaving about ¼-inch wall. Mash sardines with fork in mixing bowl. Add relish, butter, 1 egg, salt, and pepper. Mix thoroughly. Fill onions with sardine mixture. Roll onions in flour. Dip in well-beaten remaining egg, then in bread crumbs. Fry in deep fat (365° F.) 2 to 3 minutes, or until golden brown, turning frequently. *Makes 6 servings*

APPETIZER CAVIAR MOLD

1 envelope unflavored
  gelatine
½ cup water
1 tablespoon lemon juice
1½ cups dairy sour cream
2 containers (4 ounces each)
  red caviar

4 hard-cooked eggs, sieved
½ teaspoon salt
¼ teaspoon Tabasco
1 tablespoon chopped chives
  or onion
Wafers or pumpernickel

Sprinkle gelatine over cold water in saucepan. Place over low heat and stir 3 minutes or until gelatine is dissolved. Remove from heat. Stir in lemon juice, sour cream, caviar, eggs, salt, and Tabasco. Beat with a rotary beater until caviar is broken up. Stir in chives or onion. Turn into 4-cup mold. Chill until firm. Serve with crisp wafers or pumpernickel. *Makes 32 servings*

EGGS MIMOSA

6 hard-cooked eggs
1 can (2 ounces) pâté de foie
2 tablespoons mayonnaise

Cut eggs in half lengthwise and remove yolks. Reserve yolks. Refill whites with pâté and arrange on serving dish. Cover each egg with 1 teaspoon mayonnaise. Sieve egg yolk and sprinkle as garnish over eggs. *Makes 12*

STUFFED EGGS

12 hard-cooked eggs
1 cup cooked crab meat,
 flaked
1 cup finely chopped celery
2 tablespoons finely chopped
 green pepper

1 tablespoon French salad
 dressing mix
⅓ cup dairy sour cream

Cut eggs in half lengthwise. Remove yolks and mash in mixing bowl. Combine egg yolks, crab meat, celery, green pepper, salad dressing mix, and sour cream. Blend well. Refill egg whites. Chill until ready to use. *Makes 24*

EGG HEADS

12 hard-cooked eggs
1 package (3 ounces)
 cream cheese, softened
1 tablespoon prepared
 mustard
1 tablespoon oil and vinegar
 dressing

1 tablespoon Worcestershire
 sauce
½ teaspoon salt
6 large black olives, pitted
12 stuffed green olives
Pimiento

Cut eggs in half, crosswise. Remove yolks. Mash yolks in mixing bowl with cream cheese, blending until smooth. Blend in mustard, oil and vinegar dressing, Worcestershire sauce, and salt. Refill egg whites; put two halves together; fasten with toothpicks lengthwise, leaving some toothpick extending on top. Make collars ½-inch wide and 6 inches in length from sturdy white paper. Fasten ends together with staple or paper clip. Stand eggs in collars. Put one half black olive on end of toothpick for cap. Slice stuffed olives for eyes, using a little pimiento for nose and mouth. *Makes 12*

EASTER CHEESE "CIRAK"

1 quart milk	**Dash cayenne**
12 eggs	**Horseradish or pickled beets**
1 tablespoon sugar	**Crackers**
½ teaspoon salt	

Heat milk in top of large double boiler. Break eggs into milk, one at a time, stirring constantly, making sure that each yolk is broken. Add sugar, salt, and cayenne. Cook over simmering water, stirring constantly, until mixture looks like scrambled eggs. Double enough cheesecloth to set into a sieve and have sufficient overlap to tie corners together. Pour hot mixture into sieve. Gather opposite corners of cheesecloth together and tie tightly. Hang and allow to drain 1 hour. When cold and set, remove cirak from cheesecloth. Cover and place in refrigerator. Chill thoroughly until ready to use. Slice or cut into wedges. Serve with horseradish or pickled beets on crisp crackers. *Makes 1 cheese*

DEVILED EGGS DELUXE

6 hard-cooked eggs	¼ teaspoon salt
3 tablespoons mayonnaise	⅛ teaspoon pepper
2 teaspoons prepared mustard	Parsley
2 teaspoons lemon juice	Paprika
1½ teaspoons Worcestershire sauce	

Cut eggs in half lengthwise. Remove yolks. Mash yolks in mixing bowl. Combine yolks with mayonnaise, mustard, lemon juice, Worcestershire sauce, salt, and pepper. Blend well. Refill egg whites. Garnish with parsley; sprinkle with paprika. *Makes 12*

VARIATIONS

TUNA DEVILED EGGS

½ cup dairy sour cream
½ cup flaked tuna
⅛ teaspoon curry powder

Follow recipe above, substituting sour cream for mayonnaise. Blend in tuna and curry powder.

BACON DEVILED EGGS

Follow recipe above, adding 8 slices of crumbled, cooked bacon to yolk mixture.

HAM DEVILED EGGS

Follow recipe above, adding 1 can (2¼ ounces) deviled ham to yolk mixture.

CHEESE DEVILED EGGS

Follow recipe above, adding ⅔ cup grated sharp Cheddar cheese and 2 tablespoons additional mayonnaise to egg yolk mixture.

ATHENIAN MUSHROOMS

½ **pound small mushrooms**	1 **teaspoon salt**
½ **cup lemon juice**	1 **teaspoon crushed tarragon**
⅔ **cup olive oil**	**leaves**
½ **teaspoon Tabasco**	

Wipe mushrooms with a damp cloth. Trim off bottom of stem and cut in half lengthwise. Combine remaining ingredients in mixing bowl and pour over mushrooms. Marinate in the refrigerator overnight. Drain before serving. *Makes 2 cups*

MUSHROOMS A LA GRECQUE

1 pound fresh mushrooms or 2 cans (4 ounces each) buttons, drained	1 teaspoon tarragon
	2 bay leaves
	1 clove garlic, minced
½ teaspoon salt	½ cup olive oil
Pepper to taste	2 tablespoons lemon juice

Trim, wash, and drain mushrooms. Place in mixing bowl and add all remaining ingredients except lemon juice. Mix well and refrigerate 12 hours. Turn into saucepan and simmer 10 minutes. Chill thoroughly. Add lemon juice just before serving. *Makes 6 servings*

MUSHROOM APPETIZER

½ pound small mushrooms	½ teaspoon Tabasco
⅓ cup olive oil	Pinch thyme
3 tablespoons wine vinegar	2 cups water
2 tablespoons lemon juice	3 tablespoons finely chopped parsley
¾ teaspoon salt	

Wipe mushrooms with damp cloth. Trim off bottom of stem and cut in half lengthwise. Combine olive oil, wine vinegar, lemon juice, salt, Tabasco, thyme, and water in small saucepan. Bring to boil. Simmer 5 minutes to blend flavors. Add mushrooms to boiling liquid. Cook slowly over low heat 5 minutes or until barely tender. Let cool in liquid. Add chopped parsley and chill. Drain well before serving. *Makes 3 cups*

CURRIED MUSHROOM ROLLS

12 to 14 thin slices bread
Butter or margarine, softened
2 tablespoons butter or margarine
½ pound fresh mushrooms, finely chopped
½ teaspoon curry powder

1 tablespoon fresh lemon juice
½ teaspoon salt
¹⁄₁₆ teaspoon ground black pepper
¹⁄₁₆ teaspoon ground cayenne pepper

Trim crust from bread slices and roll to ⅛ inch thickness with rolling pin. (This step is important to prevent bread from breaking when making it into a roll.) Spread surface of each bread slice thinly with softened butter and reserve for later use. Heat 2 tablespoons butter in skillet and sauté mushrooms until tender. Season with curry powder and add lemon juice. Add remaining seasonings. Spread about 1 tablespoon mushroom mixture over each slice buttered bread. Roll up as for jelly roll. Fasten ends with toothpicks. Place on greased baking sheets. Brush lightly with melted butter and bake in 425° F. oven 10 minutes or until brown. (Cut into 2 pieces to serve.) *Makes 24 to 28*

LAMB-STUFFED MUSHROOMS

1 pound ground lamb	**⅓ cup mayonnaise**
1 tablespoon finely chopped onion	**¼ teaspoon salt**
	⅛ teaspoon pepper
1 tablespoon prepared horseradish	**⅛ teaspoon basil**
	1½ pounds fresh mushrooms
1 teaspoon prepared mustard	

Combine all ingredients except mushrooms in mixing bowl. Blend well. Remove stems from mushrooms. Fill mushroom caps with lamb mixture. Place in greased shallow baking dish. Bake in 350° F. oven 25 minutes or until done. *Makes about 36*

CUCUMBERS VINAIGRETTE

2 large or 3 small cucumbers	**3 tablespoons olive oil**
1 tablespoon salt	**¼ teaspoon Tabasco**
¼ cup vinegar	**Chopped green onion**

Peel cucumbers, slice very thin, place in bowl, and sprinkle with salt. Let stand 1 hour, then drain, squeezing liquid from cucumbers. Add vinegar, oil, and Tabasco and toss gently. Chill. Sprinkle with chopped green onion. *Makes 4 servings*

MEDITERRANEAN EGGPLANT APPETIZER

1 small eggplant
½ cup butter or margarine
¼ cup fresh lemon juice
2 tablespoons minced parsley
½ teaspoon minced garlic
1 cup finely chopped green pepper

1½ teaspoons salt
⅛ teaspoon ground black pepper
¼ cup olive or salad oil
½ cup yogurt or thick dairy sour cream
Thinly sliced white bread

Peel eggplant and cut in half lengthwise, then cut into cross-wise slices as thin as possible. Melt butter in heavy skillet. Add eggplant slices and sauté 3 to 4 minutes on both sides until tender. Set aside on absorbent paper 1 hour or until cool. Combine remaining ingredients except bread in mixing bowl. Add eggplant slices, a few at a time. Chill and serve on bread slices. *Makes about 24*

EGGPLANT APPETIZER

1 small eggplant
⅓ cup olive oil
½ teaspoon Tabasco

½ teaspoon salt
¼ cup lemon juice
1 small onion, chopped

Wash and peel eggplant. Slice in fine strips about 2 inches long. Make marinade by combining olive oil, Tabasco, salt, lemon juice, and onion in mixing bowl. Add eggplant strips. Chill. *Makes 2 cups*

STUFFED ARTICHOKE HEARTS

2 cans (14 ounces each) artichoke hearts, drained	**Mayonnaise**
Yolks of 6 hard-cooked eggs	**Salt and pepper to taste**
2 teaspoons tarragon vinegar	**Minced parsley and tiny pieces of fresh tomato for garnish**
1 tablespoon minced parsley	

Rinse artichoke hearts with cold water. Drain and pat dry. Reserve. Sieve egg yolks into mixing bowl. Blend crumbled egg yolk with vinegar and 1 tablespoon minced parsley. Stir in enough mayonnaise to bind mixture. Add salt and pepper to taste. Pile mixture on top of artichoke hearts. Sprinkle with minced parsley and garnish with pieces of fresh tomato. Chill until ready to serve. *Makes 18*

MARINATED FRENCH ARTICHOKE HEARTS

2 tablespoons wine vinegar	**Pinch garlic powder**
1 tablespoon olive oil	**2 cans (14 ounces each) artichoke hearts**
1 teaspoon sugar	
¼ teaspoon tarragon leaves	**2 cans (2 ounces each) rolled anchovy fillets**
¼ teaspoon salt	
¼ teaspoon powdered mustard	

Combine vinegar, oil, sugar, tarragon leaves, salt, mustard, and garlic powder in saucepan. Bring to boil. Drain artichokes. Add to sauce and mix well. Cover and refrigerate overnight or until ready to use. Serve drained and topped with rolled anchovy. *Makes 18 servings*

ARTICHOKE APPETIZER

¾ cup olive oil	4 tablespoons lemon juice
¼ cup wine vinegar	1 can (15 ounces) artichoke
¾ teaspoon salt	hearts
½ teaspoon Tabasco	Artichoke leaves for garnish
1 garlic clove, peeled	if desired

Combine olive oil, vinegar, salt, Tabasco, garlic clove, and lemon juice in mixing bowl. Add artichoke hearts and chill in refrigerator until ready to use. If desired, garnish with artichoke leaves. *Makes about 2 cups*

GUACAMOLE

2 very ripe medium-sized	1 tablespoon lemon or lime
avocados	juice
1 small tomato, chopped	½ teaspoon Tabasco
1 small onion, chopped	¼ teaspoon salt

Mash avocados, in mixing bowl, leaving some pieces chunky. Add remaining ingredients. Cover immediately with protective wrap to prevent discoloration. Serve with cauliflower clusters, pepper strips, celery sticks, bacon curls, or tortillas. *Makes 3 cups*

DANISH BLUE CHEESE MOLD

½ cup cold milk	¼ teaspoon Tabasco
2 envelopes unflavored gelatine	1 shallot, sliced
	1 cup parsley leaves
1 cup milk, heated to boiling	¼ cup lemon juice
6 ounces Danish blue cheese, cut in pieces	1½ cups heavy cream
	Parsley
½ teaspoon salt	Cherry tomatoes

Put cold milk and gelatine in blender container. Cover and process on low to soften gelatine. Add boiling milk. Process until gelatine dissolves. If gelatine granules cling to container, use rubber spatula to scrape sides and push granules into center. When gelatine is dissolved, turn control to high and add remaining ingredients except parsley and tomatoes. Process until smooth. Turn into 4-cup mold. Chill until firm. Unmold and garnish with parsley and cherry tomatoes. *Makes 8 servings*

SNAPPY SNACKS

1 roll (6 ounces) sharp processed cheese	Dash cayenne
	½ teaspoon chili powder
¼ cup butter or margarine	⅓ cup finely chopped ripe olives
1 cup flour	

Combine all ingredients in mixing bowl. Blend thoroughly. Roll into ½-inch balls. Bake in a 400° F. oven 10 minutes. *Makes 36*

PARMESAN CHEESE BALLS

2 slices white bread, crusts
  removed
½ cup milk, scalded
⅔ cup grated Parmesan
  cheese
1 teaspoon flour

1 egg
Pinch cayenne
1 tablespoon bread crumbs
  or cracker meal, if needed
Fat for frying

Place white bread in saucepan. Pour scalded milk over bread and set aside until lukewarm. Place pan over low heat and stir until pasty. Remove from heat. Mix in cheese and flour. Blend egg into mixture. Add cayenne. If consistency seems too moist, add 1 tablespoon bread crumbs or cracker meal. Allow mixture to cool. Make into ¾-inch balls and deep fry in fat (350° F.) until golden brown. *Makes 25*

CHEESE BUNS

12 frozen brioches
1 package (8 ounces) Port
  Salut or Bonbel

Defrost brioches. Remove round ball at top of each and cut deep slit in center of each brioche. Cut cheese in 6 wedges. Cut each wedge in half lengthwise. Push wedge of cheese into each slit and place all brioches on ungreased cooky sheet. Replace round balls at top of brioches. Fasten in place with toothpicks. Bake in a 350° F. oven 8 to 10 minutes or until cheese is melted. Remove toothpicks and serve immediately. *Makes 12*

PRETZEL CHEESE BALLS

2 packages (3 ounces each) cream cheese, softened
1 tablespoon Worcestershire sauce
¾ cup finely crushed pretzels

Blend cheese with Worcestershire sauce in mixing bowl. Mix well. Form into 1-inch balls. Roll in crushed pretzel crumbs and serve on food picks. *Makes about 16*

PIMIENTO AND DANISH BLUE CHEESE STUFFED CELERY

½ cup Danish blue cheese
1 package (3 ounces) pimiento cream cheese
¼ teaspoon salt
2 tablespoons milk or cream

6 ribs celery, each 9 inches long
Paprika
Chopped parsley

Mix first 4 ingredients together in mixing bowl until creamy. Wash celery, cut into 3-inch pieces, and fill with cheese mixture. Garnish with paprika or chopped fresh parsley. *Makes 18*

RACLETTE OF CAMEMBERT CHEESE

1 wheel (8 ounces)
Camembert, well chilled
French bread, thinly sliced

Thoroughly chill whole 8 ounces of Camembert. Remove top crust. Place cheese on triple-fold of aluminum foil and crumple edges of foil around cheese to form flat pan. Place cheese under broiler, cut side up, about 3 inches from source of heat. Broil about 1 minute or just until top surface of cheese is soft and melted. Remove cheese from broiler. To spread melted cheese, scrape across top with serving knife and spread on thin slices of French bread. Replace cheese in broiler and repeat melting and scraping processes until cheese is completely utilized. Raise broiler pan as cheese gets smaller to keep cut surface 3 inches from source of heat. Serve immediately. *Makes 8 servings*

QUICHE DANISH BLUE

1 9-inch unbaked pastry
shell
¼ cup crumbled Danish
blue cheese
5 eggs, slightly beaten
1 cup milk

1 cup cream
¼ cup dairy sour cream
½ teaspoon salt
¼ teaspoon pepper
¼ teaspoon grated nutmeg

Line 9-inch pie plate with pastry shell and bake in a 450° F. oven 5 minutes. Sprinkle bottom of shell with Danish blue cheese. Combine eggs, milk, cream, sour cream, salt, pepper, and nutmeg in mixing bowl. Blend well. Pour over cheese. Bake in a 450° F. oven 15 minutes. Reduce heat to 350° F. and bake 10 minutes more or until custard is set. Cut in wedges and serve hot. *Makes 6 to 8 servings or 16 wedges*

QUICHE LORRAINE

1 tablespoon soft butter or margarine	¾ teaspoon salt
	⅛ teaspoon nutmeg
1 9-inch unbaked pie shell, well chilled	⅛ teaspoon sugar
	½ teaspoon Tabasco
6 slices bacon	1 cup (¼ pound) grated Swiss cheese
4 eggs	
2 cups heavy cream	

Spread butter over surface of unbaked pie shell. Cook bacon in skillet until crisp. Drain on absorbent paper. Crumble into small pieces and reserve. Combine eggs, cream, salt, nutmeg, sugar, and Tabasco in mixing bowl. Beat just long enough to mix thoroughly. Sprinkle pie shell with bacon and cheese. Pour in cream mixture. Bake in a 425° F. oven 15 minutes. Reduce oven heat to 300° F. and bake 40 minutes more, or until point of knife inserted in center comes out clean. Cut in wedges and serve at once. *Makes 6 servings*

SPICY ONION PIE

1 9-inch unbaked pastry shell
3 eggs
½ cup milk
½ cup light cream
¾ teaspoon salt
½ teaspoon Tabasco
⅛ teaspoon nutmeg

¼ pound Gruyère cheese, grated
¼ pound Swiss cheese, grated
1 tablespoon flour
1 large onion, thinly sliced and cut into quarters

Prick bottom and sides of pastry shell with fork. Bake in 450° F. oven 10 minutes or until delicate brown. Beat together eggs, milk, cream, salt, Tabasco, and nutmeg in mixing bowl. Combine grated cheese and flour. Sprinkle evenly in pastry shell. Pour in cream mixture. Top with quartered onion slices. Bake in 400° F. oven 15 minutes. Reduce heat to 325° F. and bake 30 minutes more or until point of knife inserted in center comes out clean. Cut into wedges and serve hot. *Makes 6 servings*

APPETIZER CHEESE PIE

6 slices bacon
½ cup chopped onion
4 eggs
1 can (14½ ounces) evaporated milk
⅔ cup water
¾ teaspoon salt
1 teaspoon dry mustard

½ teaspoon Tabasco
½ teaspoon paprika
1 teaspoon Worcestershire sauce
1 9-inch unbaked pastry shell
1 cup grated Cheddar cheese

Cook bacon in skillet until crisp. Drain on absorbent paper. Crumble into small pieces and reserve. Drain all but 1 tablespoon of bacon fat. Add onion to fat in skillet and cook over low heat until tender but not brown. Remove onion from pan and reserve. Combine eggs, evaporated milk, water, salt, dry mustard, Tabasco, paprika, and Worcestershire sauce in mixing bowl and beat just long enough to mix thoroughly. Sprinkle pastry shell with bacon, onion, and cheese. Pour in milk mixture. Bake in 325° F. oven 1 hour, or until point of knife inserted in center comes out clean. Let stand 5 to 10 minutes before serving. Cut into wedges and serve hot. *Makes 6 to 8 servings*

TOMATO AND OLIVE PIE

- **1 9-inch unbaked pastry shell**
- **5 tablespoons Parmesan cheese, divided**
- **2 tablespoons butter or margarine**
- **1½ cups sliced Spanish onion**
- **2 cups diced tomatoes**
- **3½ teaspoons oregano**
- **½ teaspoon crumbled rosemary**
- **⅛ teaspoon garlic powder**
- **⅛ teaspoon ground black pepper**
- **¼ cup sliced ripe olives**
- **2 cans anchovy fillets, drained**
- **9 green stuffed olives, cut in thirds**
- **Olive oil**

Sprinkle pastry shell with 3 tablespoons grated Parmesan. Heat butter in skillet and sauté onions until brown. Cool and place on top of cheese in bottom of pastry shell. Place tomatoes, oregano, rosemary, garlic powder, black pepper, and ripe olives in skillet and cook until excess moisture has evaporated. Spread over onions. Sprinkle 2 tablespoons Parmesan cheese over tomato mixture. Arrange anchovy fillets in lattice style. Place slices of stuffed olives in center of each square of lattice work. Brush olives with olive oil and bake in a 375° F. oven 30 minutes. Brush olives again with oil, cut pie into wedges, and serve hot. *Makes 6 to 8 servings*

COULOMMIERS TARTELETTES

3 tablespoons butter	**Salt and pepper to taste**
1 onion, diced	**1 9-inch pastry shell**
1 green pepper, diced	**Coulommiers cheese, cut in**
2 cloves garlic, minced	**½-inch cubes**
¼ teaspoon thyme	

Melt butter in skillet. Add onion, green pepper, garlic, and thyme and sauté until green pepper is tender. Remove from heat. Roll pastry dough very thin on floured board and sprinkle with salt and pepper. Cut dough in 2-inch squares. Place small amount of sautéed mixture and cubed cheese on each square. Fold over at corners and seal edges with fork. Place on ungreased cooky sheet and bake in 450° F. oven until crust is golden brown. *Makes 10 to 12*

COCKTAIL TARTLETS

1⅓ cups sifted all-purpose
  flour
½ teaspoon salt
½ cup shortening
2 to 3 tablespoons cold
  water
¼ cup bacon drippings
2 cans (4 ounces each)
  mushrooms, drained

1 package (1 pound) bacon,
  cooked and crumbled
1 tablespoon paprika
2 tablespoons chopped chives
2 tablespoons chopped
  parsley
2 tablespoons lemon juice
1 cup cream

Sift flour and salt together into mixing bowl. Cut in shortening with pastry blender until particles are the size of peas. Sprinkle water, a teaspoonful at a time, over small portion of flour. Mix lightly with fork and push aside. Do not rework. Repeat until all flour is moistened. Press dough into ball. Roll out ⅛ inch thick and cut in 3-inch circles. Line 2-inch muffin pans with pastry. Heat bacon drippings in skillet and sauté mushrooms. Add bacon, paprika, chives, parsley, and lemon juice to pan. Simmer 5 minutes. Blend in cream. Fill pastry shells about ⅔ full. Bake in 350° F. oven 20 to 25 minutes or until pastry is golden brown. *Makes about 30*

INDIVIDUAL PIZZAS

¼ cup shortening

½ cup milk, scalded

1 package dry or 1 cake compressed yeast

1½ cups sifted enriched flour

½ teaspoon salt

Topping*

Grease 2 cooky sheets. Add shortening to scalded milk and cool to lukewarm. Add crumbled yeast and let soften about 10 minutes. Add flour and salt and mix thoroughly. Knead dough about 5 minutes. Place on greased baking sheet. Cover with towel and let stand in warm place until double in size. Punch down and pat to ¼ inch thickness. Using a biscuit cutter, cut eighteen 2¾-inch rounds. Prepare Topping*. *Makes 18*

TOPPING

½ pound hard salami

¼ teaspoon sweet basil

¼ teaspoon oregano

¼ teaspoon salt

1 can (2½ ounces) mushroom stems and pieces, chopped

1 can (6 ounces) tomato paste

¾ cup grated American cheese

¼ cup grated Parmesan cheese

Cut salami into small pieces. Combine basil, oregano, salt, and chopped mushrooms with tomato paste in mixing bowl. Blend well. Spread sauce evenly over rounds of dough. Sprinkle small pieces of salami over sauce. Top rounds with grated cheeses. Bake in 400° F oven 15 to 20 minutes.

PETITE APPETIZER PUFFS

1 cup water
½ cup butter or margarine
1 cup sifted enriched flour
Dash salt
4 eggs

½ cup finely chopped dried beef
¼ cup grated Parmesan or Romano cheese

Combine water and butter in heavy saucepan and bring to boil, stirring constantly until butter melts. Add flour and salt all at once. Reduce heat. Cook 1 to 2 minutes, stirring constantly until mixture is smooth and forms soft ball. Remove from heat. Cool slightly. Add eggs, one at a time, beating well after each addition, until batter is smooth and shiny. Turn half of batter into mixing bowl. Stir dried beef into half of batter. Stir cheese into remaining half. Drop by level teaspoonfuls onto lightly greased baking sheet. Bake in 400° F. oven 20 to 25 minutes, or until golden brown. Serve warm with favorite dip. *Makes 108*

MEXICALI APPETIZERS

3 cups sifted enriched flour
2 teaspoons chili powder
1½ teaspoons salt
1 cup shortening
6 to 12 tablespoons cold
   water
1 tablespoon butter or
   margarine

¼ cup finely chopped onion
¼ cup finely chopped green
   pepper
1 clove garlic, crushed
½ pound ground beef
⅓ cup catsup
2 tablespoons enriched flour
1 teaspoon chili powder

Sift together 3 cups flour, 2 teaspoons chili powder, and salt
into large mixing bowl. Cut in shortening until particles are
the size of small peas. Sprinkle with water, a little at a time,
mixing lightly until dough begins to stick together. Shape into
ball. Wrap in waxed paper. Refrigerate. Meanwhile, melt
butter in saucepan. Add onion, green pepper, and garlic.
Sauté 5 minutes over low heat. Stir in beef and cook until
brown. Blend in catsup, 2 tablespoons flour, and 1 teaspoon
chili powder. Cook, over low heat, stirring constantly, until
mixture thickens. Remove from heat. Divide refrigerated dough
in half. Roll out half of dough on lightly floured board about
¹⁄₁₆ inch thick. Using 2-inch cooky cutter make 60 circles.
Place on ungreased baking sheet. Spoon 1 level teaspoonful
filling in center of each circle, spreading slightly. Repeat rolling
and cutting with second portion of dough. Cover filling with
remaining circles. Seal edges securely with fork. Bake in
400° F. oven 15 to 18 minutes, or until lightly browned. Serve
warm or cool. *Makes 60*

OLIVE TARTS

2 cups finely grated sharp natural American cheese	**¼ teaspoon Tabasco**
½ cup soft butter	**½ teaspoon salt**
1 cup sifted all-purpose flour	**1 teaspoon paprika**
	36 small stuffed olives

Blend cheese with butter. Stir in flour, Tabasco, salt, and paprika. Wrap 1 teaspoon of mixture around each olive, covering completely. Arrange on baking sheet or flat pan and freeze firm. When ready to use, spread out on baking sheet. Bake in 400° F. oven 15 minutes. Serve hot. *Makes 36*

PINEAPPLE-AVOCADO MOLD

2½ cups crushed pineapple with syrup	**½ teaspoon salt**
½ cup water	**½ teaspoon Worcestershire sauce**
1 tablespoon unflavored gelatine	**½ teaspoon onion powder**
½ cup mashed ripe avocado	**½ cup dairy sour cream**
4 teaspoons lemon juice	**¼ to ½ teaspoon dillweed**

Combine crushed pineapple, syrup, and water in saucepan. Sprinkle unflavored gelatine over pineapple to soften. Cook over low heat, stirring constantly, until gelatine dissolves. Chill until thick. Combine avocado and lemon juice in mixing bowl.

Add salt, Worcestershire sauce, and onion powder. Blend well
and stir into pineapple mixture. Turn into 4-cup mold. Chill
until set. Unmold and garnish with sour cream and dillweed.
Makes 6 servings

Canapés

CANAPE BUTTERS

Flavored butters add a special something to canapés. They may be prepared in advance and stored in the refrigerator in airtight containers. They are good when used alone as a spread for toast and flavored crackers and are excellent when they are combined with other ingredients. For best flavor results allow these butters to soften before using.

ANCHOVY BUTTER: Combine and cream together until well blended 1 tablespoon butter and ½ teaspoon anchovy paste.

ALMOND BUTTER: Finely grind 6 blanched almonds. Combine them with an equal volume of butter.

CAPER BUTTER: Blend 4 tablespoons butter with 1 tablespoon minced capers.

CAVIAR BUTTER: Blend 1 tablespoon caviar into 2 tablespoons butter.

GARLIC BUTTER: Blend 1 small crushed garlic clove into 1 tablespoon butter.

HORSERADISH BUTTER: Blend 1 teaspoon horseradish with 1 tablespoon butter.

LOBSTER BUTTER: Blend 1 tablespoon finely chopped lobster meat into 2 tablespoons butter.

SHRIMP BUTTER: Finely chop 6 shrimp. Combine and blend with 2 tablespoons butter.

TARRAGON BUTTER: Blend 1 teaspoon finely chopped tarragon with 2 tablespoons butter.

Multiply these recipes according to your needs.

SEASONED MAYONNAISE

CUCUMBER MAYONNAISE: Combine 1 cup mayonnaise with 1 cup chopped cucumber. Blend well. *Makes 1¾ cups*

CELERY MAYONNAISE: Combine 1 cup mayonnaise with ¼ cup diced celery and 2 tablespoons diced green pepper. *Makes 1¼ cups*

HORSERADISH MAYONNAISE: Combine 1 cup mayonnaise with ½ cup horseradish. *Makes about 1½ cups*

MUSTARD MAYONNAISE: Combine 1 cup mayonnaise with ⅓ cup mustard. *Makes about 1¼ cups*

TOMATO MAYONNAISE: Combine 1 cup mayonnaise with 1 cup chopped fresh tomato. *Makes about 2 cups*

AVOCADO MAYONNAISE: Combine 1 cup mayonnaise with 1 mashed ripe avocado and 1 teaspoon lemon juice. *Makes about 1¾ cups*

CHIVE MAYONNAISE: Combine 1 cup mayonnaise with 2 tablespoons chopped chives. *Makes 1 cup*

QUICK CANAPES

As a base for these delicious treats use bread that has been cut into fancy shapes, toasted, and buttered or crackers in different shapes and sizes.

1. Danish blue cheese softened with cream
2. Danish blue cheese topped with bacon strip and placed under broiler
3. Danish blue cheese with layer of sardines topped with chopped parsley
4. Hard-cooked egg yolks blended with Danish blue cheese and finely chopped gherkins, olives, and pistachio nuts
5. Hard-cooked egg yolks blended with pâté de foie and finely chopped black olives
6. Hard-cooked egg yolks blended with chopped green olives and ham, beef, or chicken
7. Hard-cooked egg yolks blended with cream cheese and anchovy paste
8. Hard-cooked egg yolks blended with capers and chopped olives and sprinkled with cinnamon
9. Chopped egg seasoned with mustard and chili sauce
10. Chopped egg mixed with mayonnaise, topped with asparagus tips, and garnished with chopped parsley
11. Chopped anchovies mixed with mayonnaise and sprinkled with chopped pistachio nuts
12. Sardine paste seasoned with lemon and chopped onion
13. Anchovy fillets topped with horseradish mixed with butter

14. Slices of pimiento on a spread of anchovy paste topped with small shrimp

15. Slices of tomato on spread of anchovy paste garnished with tiny balls of cream cheese that have been rolled in soft butter

16. Slices of cucumber on spread of anchovy paste, garnished with tiny balls of Danish blue cheese

17. Caviar spread on layer of garlic butter

18. Caviar sprinkled with chopped egg whites and finely chopped onion

19. Chopped salmon mixed with lemon juice

20. Smoked salmon on layer of minced pimiento and celery

21. Flaked cooked fish mixed with mayonnaise

22. Liverwurst mashed to a paste and seasoned with chili sauce

23. Mashed liverwurst and mayonnaise topped with thin slice of apple and sprinkled with fresh chopped chives

24. Cold meat loaf on spread of sour cream

25. Puréed ham spread with Cheddar cheese placed under broiler

26. Chopped ham mixed with finely chopped gherkins topped with cocktail onion

27. Finely minced chicken mixed with mayonnaise and curry powder

28. Finely minced chicken marinated in French dressing and seasoned with ginger

29. Finely minced chicken, pimiento, and apples blended with mayonnaise

30. Liver and bacon ground together and seasoned with garlic salt

31. Baked beans mashed and seasoned with horseradish

32. Chopped olives blended with mayonnaise
33. Peanut butter with chopped pickle
34. Peanut butter with chopped onion
35. Chopped marinated mushrooms that have been mixed with mayonnaise and mustard
36. Thin slices of green pepper on a spread of cream cheese garnished with sliced olives
37. Sliced artichoke hearts marinated in French dressing and garnished with diced shrimp that have been mixed with mayonnaise
38. Sliced artichoke hearts on spread of anchovy paste topped with caviar
39. Cream cheese seasoned with garlic and garnished with parsley
40. Cream cheese mixed with chopped watercress and garnished with walnut halves

CRAB ASPIC CANAPES

1 cup mayonnaise
1 tablespoon lemon juice
1 tablespoon horseradish
⅓ cup finely chopped parsley
⅓ cup finely chopped scallions
½ teaspoon dry mustard
½ teaspoon dried tarragon
¼ teaspoon Tabasco
2 cans (5 to 7 ounces each) crab meat, drained, chilled
Pimiento
Ripe olives
1 envelope unflavored gelatine
½ cup cold consommé
Melba toast rounds

Combine first 8 ingredients in mixing bowl. Mix well. Arrange small bite-size mounds of crab meat on baking sheet. Chill briefly. Garnish with tiny decorative pieces of pimiento and olives. In a saucepan, sprinkle gelatine over consommé to soften. Place over low heat, and cook, stirring constantly, until gelatine dissolves. Stir into mayonnaise mixture. Mix well. Cover seafood mounds one at a time with gelatine-mayonnaise mixture and decorate each mound with pimiento or olive. Chill. To serve place on Melba toast rounds using a spatula. *Makes 25 to 30*

VARIATIONS OF CRAB ASPIC CANAPES

SALMON ASPIC CANAPES: Use 1 can (1 pound) red salmon as a substitute for crab meat

SHRIMP ASPIC CANAPES: Use 2 cans (4½ to 5 ounces each) jumbo shrimp as a substitute for crab meat

TUNA ASPIC CANAPES: Use 2 cans (7 ounces each) tuna as a substitute for crab meat

BAMBINOS

1 jar (5 ounces) olive and pimiento cheese spread

½ clove garlic, finely minced

5 to 6 scallions

1 can (4 ounces) pimientos, drained

18 finger rolls (hard or soft poppy seed)

8 to 10 medium radishes, thinly sliced

4 cans (4 ounces each) sardines, drained

Blend cheese spread with garlic in mixing bowl. Refrigerate until ready to use. Peel and wash scallions and cut into four to six pieces lengthwise, then one-inch pieces crosswise. Slice pimientos into thin slivers. Slice finger rolls almost in two, leaving a hinge. Spread with cheese mixture. Over this place a layer of radishes. Next, the whole sardine, one to a roll. Top with scallions and pimientos. Close rolls. For canapés, cut in half crosswise with sharp knife, but arrange with halves remaining together. Wrap in transparent plastic wrap and chill until ready to use. If desired, skewer each portion with food pick. *Makes 36*

SALMA GUNDY

¾ **pound salt herring**	**2 tablespoons salad oil**
Water	**40 bread rounds, 1½ inches**
⅓ **cup vinegar**	**in diameter**
2 teaspoons instant minced	**Butter or margarine**
onion	**Paprika**
8 whole allspice	**Parsley**
1 whole hot red pepper	

Soak herring overnight in enough water to cover. Drain, rinse well, remove all bones. Cut into ½-inch squares. Place in jar. Combine next 4 ingredients in saucepan. Bring to boil. Cook 1 minute. Remove from heat and add oil. Pour over fish in jar. Marinate at least 24 hours. Toast rounds of bread on both sides. Spread one side with butter. Top each with a square of marinated fish. Garnish with paprika and parsley. *Makes 40*

SALMON CANAPES

1 can (8 ounces) salmon

1 teaspoon grated onion

3 tablespoons mayonnaise

1½ teaspoons lemon juice

¼ teaspoon Worcestershire sauce

½ teaspoon paprika

¼ teaspoon salt

¼ teaspoon Tabasco

12 small rounds rye bread

12 pickle slices

Combine first 8 ingredients in mixing bowl. Blend well and spread on small rounds of rye bread. Top with pickle slices. *Makes 12*

ANTIPASTO TOAST

2 tablespoons olive or salad oil

½ cup chopped leeks or scallions

2 tablespoons chopped fresh parsley

½ cup chopped green pepper

½ cup chopped fresh tomatoes

¼ cup grated Parmesan cheese

1 teaspoon salt

1 teaspoon paprika

⅛ teaspoon ground black pepper

8 slices bread

2 large hard-cooked eggs

Capers

Heat oil in skillet. Add scallions, parsley, green pepper, and tomatoes and sauté in hot oil until tender. Add cheese, salt, paprika, and pepper. Toast bread slices on both sides and cut each into 3 fingers or 4 squares. Spread with antipasto mixture. Separate yolks from whites of hard-cooked eggs and chop fine in separate bowls. Sprinkle a little of each over canapés. Garnish with capers. *Makes 24–32*

SAN JUAN CANAPES

½ **pound bacon**
½ **pound Munster cheese**
2 **tablespoons instant minced onion**
2 **tablespoons water**
½ **cup chili sauce**
½ **teaspoon oregano leaves**
⅛ **teaspoon ground black pepper**
½ **teaspoon salt**
11 **slices bread**

Fry bacon crisp. Using medium blade put bacon and cheese through food chopper into mixing bowl. Soften instant minced onion in water and add to bacon-cheese mixture. Blend in chili sauce, oregano, pepper, and salt. Trim crusts from bread slices and toast on both sides. Spread toast with mixture and cut into 8 squares. Place under 350° F. broiler and broil until topping is bubbly. *Makes 88*

BEATEN BISCUIT AND HAM CANAPES

2 **cups sifted all-purpose flour**
½ **teaspoon salt**
⅓ **cup shortening**
½ **cup cold water**
Ham Filling*

Sift flour and salt together into mixing bowl. Cut in shortening until particles are the size of small peas. Stir in water. Knead dough ½ minute. Using medium blade put mixture through food chopper 8 times. Roll dough ¼ inch thick. Fold in half. Roll again to ¼ inch thickness. Shape dough into rounds with 1½-inch biscuit cutter. Bake in 350° F. oven 25 to 30 minutes or until lightly browned. Biscuits will puff and centers will be hollow. When biscuits are cold fill with ham filling. *Makes 30*

HAM FILLING

1 cup ground cooked smoked ham

2 tablespoons instant minced onion

¼ teaspoon powdered mustard

Dash ground black pepper

¼ cup dairy sour cream

Put ham through meat grinder into mixing bowl. Add remaining ingredients. Use as filling for Beaten Biscuit Canapés.

BREAD ROLLS NICOISE

1 loaf unsliced small ice box rye bread

2 packages (3 ounces each) cream cheese, softened

2 tablespoons butter

2 tablespoons cream

Pinch garlic powder

2 ounces Cheddar cheese, finely diced

⅓ cup finely diced ham

1 tablespoon chopped green pepper

1 tablespoon chopped pimiento

Split loaf of bread in half lengthwise. Hollow out center until near crust. Blend cream cheese, butter, and cream with pinch of garlic powder in mixing bowl. Add Cheddar cheese, ham, green pepper, and pimiento. Blend. Fill each hollowed half of bread with mixture. Put 2 halves together. Roll tightly in protective wrap and refrigerate until firm. Slice into ¼-inch slices before serving. *Makes 42 to 48*

FRENCH BRIE BRILLIANT

½ pound French Brie, at
   room temperature
¼ cup dairy sour cream
10 black olives, pitted,
   minced

1 tablespoon chopped chives
   or scallions
Crackers or toast fingers

Blend Brie with sour cream in mixing bowl. Add olives and chives or scallions to cheese and blend well. Chill. Remove from refrigerator 1 hour before serving. Spread on crackers or toast fingers. Place on ungreased broiling pan and broil 2 to 3 minutes or until cheese is bubbly. Serve hot. *Makes 36*

GOURMET CANAPES

½ cup deviled ham
1 can (2½ ounces) pâté
8 slices white bread cut in
   2½-inch rounds
1 teaspoon prepared mustard

2 tablespoons butter,
   softened
Truffles
Capers

Combine ham and pâté in mixing bowl. Blend until smooth. Place bread rounds on baking sheet and toast lightly on both sides in oven. Meanwhile combine mustard and butter in small mixing bowl. Blend well. Spread toasted bread rounds with mustard-butter mixture, then with pâté mixture, and garnish with slivers of truffles or capers. *Makes 16*

CANAPE MEPHISTA

1 cup shredded Cheddar cheese	1 egg yolk
⅔ cup grated Parmesan cheese	Black pepper to taste
6 tablespoons butter	10 slices bread, crusts removed

Cream cheeses and butter together in mixing bowl until smooth. Blend in egg yolk and season with pepper. Toast bread on one side. Spread cheese on toasted side. Cut each toast into 6 pieces. Place on ungreased baking sheet and place under broiler until cheese is light brown. Place in hot oven about ½ minute. Serve hot. *Makes 60*

CURRIED NUT CANAPES

1 package (3 ounces) cream cheese, softened	1 teaspoon minced onion
½ cup chopped mixed nuts	¼ teaspoon curry powder
3 slices bacon, cooked and crumbled	¼ teaspoon Worcestershire sauce
1 tablespoon milk	24 toast rounds
	Olive slices

Combine cream cheese, mixed nuts, bacon, milk, onion, curry powder, and Worcestershire sauce in mixing bowl. Blend well. Spread on toast rounds. Garnish with olive slices. Place on ungreased broiler rack and broil 1 to 2 minutes, or until thoroughly heated. Serve hot. *Makes 24*

NUTTY CHEDDAR CANAPES

⅔ cup grated sharp Cheddar cheese
⅔ cup chopped mixed nuts
¼ cup mayonnaise

2 teaspoons minced onion
1½ teaspoons Worcestershire sauce
24 toast rounds

Combine cheese, mixed nuts, mayonnaise, onion, and Worcestershire sauce in mixing bowl. Blend well. Spread on toast rounds. Place on ungreased broiler rack and broil 1 to 2 minutes, or until golden. *Makes 24*

SAVORY APPETIZER PASTRIES

1 package (9½ ounces) pie crust mix
1 can (2¼ ounces) deviled ham or liver pâté
2 or 3 tablespoons Sauterne

Turn pie crust mix into mixing bowl. Add deviled ham or liver pâté and wine. Mix lightly but thoroughly. Roll out on floured board to about ⅛ inch thickness. Cut into 2-inch rounds or 4×1-inch strips. Bake on ungreased cooky sheets in 450° F. oven 8 to 10 minutes or until lightly browned. Cool before serving. *Makes about 55*

Spreads

CALIFORNIA WALNUT PATE

1/4 cup butter or margarine
1 pound chicken livers
1/2 pound fresh mushrooms, sliced
1 tablespoon instant minced onion
1/2 teaspoon salt
1/2 teaspoon crumbled tarragon

1/8 teaspoon pepper
1 package (3 ounces) cream cheese, softened
1 cup chopped toasted walnuts
2 tablespoons bourbon
Chicken broth, if necessary

Melt butter in skillet and sauté chicken livers and mushrooms 5 minutes or until livers lose pink color. Add onion, salt, tarragon, and pepper. Cover and simmer 5 minutes. Purée 3/4 of mixture in blender or press through sieve. Finely chop remaining mixture. Combine the two. Add cream cheese and stir until smooth. Add toasted walnuts and bourbon. Blend well. If a bit dry, add small amount chicken broth. Chill until ready to use. *Makes 2 1/2 cups*

PARTY PATE

1 can (3 or 4 ounces)
  chopped mushrooms
1 enveloped unflavored
  gelatine
1 can condensed beef
  bouillon
2 tablespoons brandy

1 teaspoon Worcestershire
  sauce
2 cans (about 3¾ ounces
  each) liverwurst spread
½ cup pitted ripe olives
¼ cup parsley leaves

Drain liquid from mushrooms into blender container. Add gelatine. Cover and process at lowest speed to soften. Heat ½ cup of bouillon to boiling. Add to blender container and continue to blend until gelatine dissolves. If gelatine granules cling to container, use rubber spatula to push them into the center. Turn to highest speed, add remaining ingredients, and process until smooth. Pour into 4-cup mold or bowl and chill until firm, 4 hours or overnight. *Makes 3⅓ cups*

PIMIENTO CHICKEN LIVER SPREAD

1 can (2 ounces) pimientos,
  chopped
½ cup chopped, cooked
  chicken livers
2 hard-cooked eggs, diced
1 teaspoon chopped onion

1 teaspoon prepared mustard
Dash Worcestershire sauce
Mayonnaise or cream to
  moisten
Parsley sprigs

Blend all ingredients except parsley in mixing bowl. Garnish canapés with sprigs of parsley. *Makes ¾ cup*

SAUSAGE SPECIALTY

1 package (8 ounces)
  Braunschweiger
  liver sausage
⅔ cup minced garlic dill
  pickle
⅓ cup minced celery

2 tablespoons minced onion
1 tablespoon pickle juice
1 teaspoon lemon juice
¼ teaspoon garlic powder
⅛ teaspoon Tabasco

Cream liver sausage in mixing bowl. Add remaining ingredients and blend well. Chill until ready to use. *Makes 2 to 2¼ cups*

SNOWCAP SPREAD

2 cans (4½ ounces each)
  deviled ham
1 tablespoon minced onion
1 package (8 ounces)
  cream cheese, softened

¼ cup dairy sour cream
2½ teaspoons sharp mustard
Parsley

Combine deviled ham and minced onion in mixing bowl. Blend well and turn out on serving dish in mound. Combine cream cheese, sour cream, and mustard together in mixing bowl and use as "frosting" for ham mound. Garnish with parsley. *Makes 2¼ cups*

BACON NUT SPREAD

1 package (3 ounces) cream
  cheese, softened
1½ tablespoons salad dressing
¼ teaspoon Worcestershire
  sauce

8 slices bacon, cooked crisp
  and crumbled
4 tablespoons chopped salted
  peanuts

Blend cream cheese, salad dressing, and Worcestershire sauce in mixing bowl. Add bacon and peanuts. Mix well. Chill until ready to use. *Makes ¾ cup*

HOT TUNA MUSHROOM SPREAD

1 can (6½ or 7 ounces) tuna,
  drained
½ cup canned condensed
  cream of mushroom soup
1 tablespoon finely chopped
  canned pimiento

1 tablespoon finely chopped
  green pepper
¼ teaspoon salt
Dash paprika
Toast rounds
Grated cheese

Combine tuna, soup, pimiento, green pepper, and seasonings in saucepan. Cook, over low heat, stirring occasionally. Spread on toast rounds and sprinkle with cheese. Place on ungreased broiling pan and broil 3 to 4 inches from source of heat 5 to 7 minutes or until cheese is lightly browned. *Makes 1½ cups*

TASTE-TEMPTING SPREAD

1 can (6½ or 7 ounces) tuna, drained	1 tablespoon lemon juice
3 tablespoons mayonnaise	Salt to taste
1 tablespoon finely chopped celery	Dash Worcestershire sauce
1 tablespoon chili sauce	1 medium-sized cucumber, peeled, scored, and thinly sliced
1 tablespoon catsup	Toast rounds

Combine all ingredients except cucumber and toast rounds in mixing bowl. Blend well. Place one cucumber slice on each toast round and top with tuna mixture. Place on ungreased broiling pan and broil 3 to 4 inches from source of heat 5 to 7 minutes. Serve immediately. *Makes 1¼ cups*

TANGY SPREAD

1 can (6½ or 7 ounces) chunk-style tuna, drained	3 tablespoons mayonnaise
1 tablespoon finely chopped celery	Horseradish Butter*
	Toast rounds
	Chopped parsley

Combine tuna, celery, and mayonnaise in mixing bowl. Blend well. Spread Horseradish Butter* on toast rounds and top with tuna mixture. Garnish with parsley. *Makes 1¼ cups*

HORSERADISH BUTTER

½ cup softened butter or
 margarine
3 tablespoons prepared
 horseradish

Combine both ingredients in small mixing bowl and blend well.

JAMAICA SPREAD

1 medium-sized ripe avocado   1 teaspoon prepared
1 can (6½ or 7 ounces)   horseradish
 tuna, drained   ½ teaspoon salt
3 tablespoons lime juice

Mash avocado in mixing bowl. Add remaining ingredients.
Mix well. *Makes 1½ cups*

TUNA-PINEAPPLE CANAPE SPREAD

1 can (6½ or 7 ounces)   1 tablespoon pineapple syrup
 tuna, drained   ¼ cup chopped celery
½ cup drained canned   ¼ cup mayonnaise
 crushed pineapple   Salt to taste

Combine all ingredients in mixing bowl. Blend well. *Makes 2 cups*

WALNUT CANAPE SPREAD

½ **cup chopped walnuts**
¼ **cup mayonnaise**
1 **can (6½ or 7 ounces)**
  tuna, drained

Combine all ingredients in mixing bowl. Blend well. *Makes 1½ cups*

TUNA-AVOCADO CANAPE SPREAD

½ **medium-sized avocado,**   2 **tablespoons lemon juice**
  mashed   **Salt and pepper to taste**
1 **can (6½ or 7 ounces)**
  tuna, drained

Combine avocado, tuna, lemon juice, and salt and pepper in mixing bowl. Blend well. *Makes 1½ cups*

HOT GOURMET CANAPE

1 can (6½ or 7 ounces)
tuna, drained
3 hard-cooked eggs, chopped
3 tablespoons finely chopped
green pepper
⅓ cup chopped anchovies
1 medium-sized tomato,
chopped

¼ teaspoon Worchestershire
sauce
3 tablespoons chili sauce
3 tablespoons mayonnaise
Toast rounds

Combine all ingredients except toast rounds in mixing bowl.
Blend thoroughly. Spread on toast rounds. Place rounds on
ungreased broiling pan and broil 3 to 4 inches from source
of heat 5 minutes. Serve immediately. *Makes 2½ cups*

ASPARAGUS SHARPIES

1 cup cooked or canned
asparagus cuts and tips
1 cup grated sharp cheese
2 teaspoons prepared
mustard

1 teaspoon vinegar
1 teaspoon seasoned salt
1 teaspoon paprika
¼ cup dairy sour cream

Chop asparagus and combine with cheese in mixing bowl.
Add remaining ingredients except sour cream and beat with
electric mixer until smooth. Fold in sour cream. *Makes about
2½ cups*

TANGY SPREAD

½ cup cooked or canned
asparagus cuts and tips
1 can (2¼ ounces) deviled
ham

¼ cup pickle relish
¼ cup mayonnaise

Chop asparagus and place in mixing bowl. Add remaining ingredients and beat with electric mixer until smooth. *Makes 1¼ cups*

COUNTRY SPREAD

1 can (2¼ ounces) deviled
ham
1 package (8 ounces) cream
cheese, softened

½ cup dairy sour cream
2 tablespoons finely chopped
chives

Combine all ingredients in mixing bowl. Blend well. Refrigerate 3 hours to blend flavors before serving. Serve at room temperature. *Makes 2 cups*

ANCHOVY WINE CHEESE SPREAD

1 can (2 ounces) anchovy
fillets, drained
2 packages (8 ounces each)
cream cheese, softened

¼ cup sherry
2 tablespoons finely chopped
stuffed green olives

Mash anchovies in mixing bowl. Blend cheese into fish. Beat in sherry until mixture is smooth. Add olives. Cover and chill several hours to blend flavors before serving. Pile mixture into bowl and place bowl in cracked ice. *Makes 1½ cups*

PARTY CHEESE SPREAD

2 packages (5½ ounces each) Cheddar cheese spread
½ teaspoon grated orange rind
¼ cup dry vermouth
1 cup small curd cottage cheese

Beat Cheddar cheese with orange rind and vermouth in mixing bowl until smooth. Stir in cottage cheese. Cover and let stand an hour or longer to blend flavors. To serve attractively, fill 1 or 2 large orange shells with vermouth-cheese spread. *Makes 2 cups*

CONTINENTAL SPREAD

2 packages (3 ounces each) cream cheese, softened
¾ cup Danish blue cheese
¼ cup milk or light cream

Combine cheeses in mixing bowl and blend until smooth. Beat in milk or cream. Add more milk or cream if thinner dip is desired. *Makes 1½ cups*

CITRUS SPREAD

1 package (3 ounces)
    cream cheese, softened
 1 tablespoon lemon juice
	⅛ teaspoon mace
	 ⅛ teaspoon shredded lemon
	    peel

Combine all ingredients in mixing bowl. Blend well. Cover and chill 2 to 3 hours to blend flavors before serving. *Makes about ⅓ cup*

RADISH SPREAD

1 package (3 ounces)
    cream cheese, softened
 2 tablespoons butter or
    margarine
 ¼ teaspoon celery salt
 Dash paprika
	¼ teaspoon Worcestershire
	    sauce
	 ½ cup finely chopped radish
	 2 tablespoons finely chopped
	    green onion

Combine first 5 ingredients in mixing bowl. Beat until smooth. Add radish and onion and chill at least 2 hours to blend flavors before serving. *Makes 1½ cups*

GARLIC CHEESE SPREAD

2 tablespoons evaporated   **⅛ teaspoon garlic salt**
milk   **⅛ teaspoon Tabasco**
1 package (3 ounces)
Cheddar cheese, softened

Blend evaporated milk into cheese, a little at a time. Add
garlic salt and Tabasco. Serve at room temperature. *Makes
about ½ cup*

SNAPPY CARAWAY SPREAD

2 tablespoons evaporated   **1 teaspoon caraway seeds**
milk   **⅛ teaspoon Tabasco**
1 package (3 ounces) sharp
Cheddar cheese, softened

Blend evaporated milk into cheese, a little at a time. Add
caraway seeds and Tabasco. Serve at room temperature.
Makes about ½ cup

CHEESE BOLOGNA SPREAD

2 cups ground bologna	**¼ cup mayonnaise**
½ cup grated sharp	**Sweet pickle rounds**
Cheddar cheese	**Green onion tops**
2 tablespoons pickle relish	**Celery leaves**
1 tablespoon grated onion	

Combine bologna, cheese, pickle relish, onion, and mayonnaise in mixing bowl. Blend well. Form mixture into "pineapple" shape on serving platter. Score "pineapple" and stud with sweet pickle rounds. Insert green onion tops and celery leaves for top of pineapple. *Makes 2¾ cups*

REBLOCHON SPREAD

3 tablespoons minced parsley	**⅛ teaspoon cayenne**
2 tablespoons minced chives	**Rye or pumpernickel bread**
1 teaspoon crumbled tarragon	**Reblochon cheese**
1 cup salt butter, softened	**Grated lemon rind**
¼ teaspoon salt	

Combine parsley, chives, tarragon, and butter in mixing bowl. Cream until well blended. Stir in salt and cayenne. Spread mixture on thinly sliced rye or pumpernickel bread from which crusts have been removed. Cut bread in fingers or quarters. Top each canapé with very thin slice of reblochon cheese (crust removed) and garnish with grated lemon rind. *Makes about 1 cup*

CAMEMBERT PECAN SPREAD

1 cup salt butter, softened
¼ pound shelled pecans, finely ground
3 drops Tabasco
2 tablespoons lemon juice

Camembert cheese
Toast points
Additional chopped pecans for garnish

Soften butter in mixing bowl and cream until light and fluffy. Blend in nuts and Tabasco. Beat in lemon juice. Press entire mixture through fine sieve. Spread this on crisp toast points. Top with slice of Camembert. Garnish with additional chopped pecans. *Makes 1¼ cups*

Dips

SARDINE DIP

- 2 cans (3¼ ounces each) sardines
- 2 packages (3 ounces each) cream cheese, softened
- 1 or 2 cloves garlic, minced
- 2 tablespoons minced onion
- ¼ teaspoon salt
- 2 tablespoons Worcestershire sauce
- 4 drops Tabasco
- ¼ teaspoon celery salt
- 1 tablespoon lemon juice
- Pimiento strips

Mash sardines and cream cheese thoroughly in mixing bowl. Blend well. Add all other ingredients except pimiento. Chill for several hours to blend flavors. Turn out into serving bowl and garnish with pimiento. *Makes 2 cups*

TUNA CREAM DIP

- 1 can (6½ or 7 ounces) tuna, drained
- 1 tablespoon prepared horseradish
- 1½ teaspoons onion salt
- 1 teaspoon Worcestershire sauce
- 1 cup dairy sour cream
- Chopped parsley

Combine all ingredients except sour cream and parsley in mixing bowl. Mix thoroughly. Fold in sour cream. Turn out into serving dish and garnish with chopped parsley. *Makes 2 cups*

LOBSTER CURRY DIP

1 package (8 ounces)
   cream cheese, softened
⅓ cup mayonnaise
1 tablespoon grated onion
1 to 2 teaspoons curry
   powder
1 teaspoon lemon juice
¼ teaspoon salt
1 can (5 or 6 ounces)
   lobster meat, drained,
   flaked
French fries

Blend first 6 ingredients together in mixing bowl until fluffy and smooth. Fold in lobster. Stir well. Serve with crisp french fries. *Makes about 1½ cups*

CRAB CHEESE DIP

1 can frozen condensed
   cream of shrimp soup
1 package (½ pound)
   processed cheese spread
1 egg yolk, beaten
1 can (6½ ounces) crab
   meat, drained and
   chopped
1 to 2 tablespoons sherry
Crackers

Combine soup and cheese in saucepan and cook over low heat until melted. Stir small amount of hot mixture into beaten egg yolk. Return to hot mixture. Cook, stirring constantly, until thick. Stir in crab and mix well. Blend in sherry. Serve warm with crackers. *Makes about 2½ cups*

SHRIMP DIP

- 2 cups dairy sour cream
- 1 package (3 ounces) cream cheese, softened
- 1 teaspoon prepared horseradish
- 1 teaspoon chopped chives
- ½ teaspoon salt
- ½ teaspoon Worcestershire sauce
- ½ teaspoon onion salt
- ¼ teaspoon celery
- 1 pound fresh shrimp, cooked, cleaned, deveined, chopped
- French fries

Combine all ingredients in mixing bowl. Blend well. Chill 1 hour before serving. Serve with crisp french fries. *Makes 4½ cups*

VARIATIONS OF SHRIMP DIP

SMOKY SHRIMP DIP: Blend 3 to 4 drops liquid smoke into 1 cup Shrimp Dip*

CURRIED SHRIMP DIP: Blend ⅛ teaspoon (or more) curry powder into 1 cup Shrimp Dip*

BARBECUE SHRIMP DIP: Mix ¼ teaspoon (or more) barbecue seasoning into 1 cup Shrimp Dip*

SHRIMP DIP WALTER

1 cup cooked shrimp,
  mashed
1 package (3 ounces) cream
  cheese, softened
⅓ cup dairy sour cream
¼ cup minced dill pickle

¼ cup minced pimiento
½ teaspoon salt
1 teaspoon paprika
½ teaspoon vinegar
3 drops Tabasco

Combine and blend all ingredients together in large mixing bowl. Remove to serving dish. Chill well before serving. *Makes 2 cups*

CREAMY ANCHOVY DIP

1 can (2 ounces) anchovy
  fillets
Salad oil
½ cup evaporated milk
¼ cup wine vinegar

1 teaspoon salt
¼ teaspoon pepper
Dash garlic salt
½ cup coarsely snipped
  parsley

Drain oil of anchovies into measuring cup (about 1½ tablespoons). Add salad oil to make ½ cup. Pour into blender container. Add anchovies. Add remaining ingredients. Process a few seconds until smooth. Pour into serving dish. Cover and chill until ready to use. *Makes 1 cup*

MINCED CLAM DIP

1 package (3 ounces)
cream cheese, softened
1 can (7 ounces) minced
clams, drained
¼ teaspoon soy sauce

¼ teaspoon grated lemon
peel
2 teaspoons fresh lemon
juice
Pinch garlic powder

Beat cream cheese until smooth in mixing bowl. Blend in remaining ingredients. Chill until ready to use. *Makes ⅔ cup*

AVERY ISLAND CLAM DIP

2 packages (3 ounces each)
cream cheese, softened
1 teaspoon salt
½ teaspoon Tabasco
1 tablespoon grated onion

1 can (7½ ounces) clams
1 cup (8 ounces) dairy
sour cream
Olives for garnish if desired

Combine cream cheese, salt, Tabasco, and onion in mixing bowl. Blend thoroughly. Mince clams, reserving large pieces for garnish, if desired. Add clams with 2 teaspoons clam liquor to cream cheese mixture. Stir in sour cream. Turn into serving dish and chill at least ½ hour before serving. Garnish with sliced olives, if desired. *Makes 2 cups*

BACON 'N' EGG DIP

1 can (6 ounces) tomato
  paste
½ cup mayonnaise
3 hard-cooked eggs
½ pound sliced bacon,
  fried crisp, drained

¼ medium-sized green
  pepper
¼ teaspoon salt
Dash pepper
Dash Tabasco

Measure all ingredients into blender container. Process at low speed until smooth. Stop motor, if necessary, during blending to scrape down sides of container with rubber spatula. *Makes 2 cups*

PINK CONFETTI HAM DIP

1 package (8 ounces)
  cream cheese, softened
½ cup mayonnaise
2 tablespoons chili sauce
Dash pepper
¼ teaspoon celery salt

½ cup finely chopped ham
1 tablespoon minced parsley
2 tablespoons chopped
  pimiento
Salt to taste
French fries

Blend first 5 ingredients together in mixing bowl until smooth and fluffy. Fold in ham, parsley, and pimiento. Add salt. Mix well. Serve with crisp french fries. *Makes 1¾ cups*

PATIO PERFECT DIP

½ cup cooked or canned
   asparagus cuts and tips
2 tablespoons butter or
   margarine
¼ teaspoon garlic powder

1 teaspoon lemon juice
¼ cup crumbled Danish
   blue cheese
¼ cup dairy sour cream

Place all ingredients except sour cream in mixing bowl. Blend with electric mixer until smooth. Fold in sour cream. Serve at room temperature. *Makes 1½ cups*

SPRING PARTY DIP

1 cup cottage cheese
¼ cup grated radish
¼ cup grated carrot

1 teaspoon horseradish
1 tablespoon chopped chives
½ teaspoon salt

Place ingredients in blender container. Cover and process on low. Then run on high speed until smooth. *Makes about 1¼ cups*

CREAMY BLUE CHEESE DIP

1 package (8 ounces)
cream cheese, softened
3 ounces Danish blue
cheese, softened
3 tablespoons cream

2 teaspoons chopped chives
½ teaspoon Worcestershire
sauce
Paprika

Blend cheeses together in mixing bowl until smooth. Add cream, chives, and Worcestershire sauce. Blend well. Turn out into serving dish and dust with paprika. *Makes about 1¼ cups*

CHAFING DISH DIP

½ pound processed American
cheese
2 cans (4½ ounces each)
deviled ham

2 teaspoons prepared mustard
2 teaspoons Worcestershire
sauce

Melt cheese in saucepan over low heat. Stir in remaining ingredients. Turn out into chafing dish and keep hot while serving. *Makes 3½ cups*

COUNTRY CHEESE DIP

1 cup finely shredded, sharp
   Cheddar cheese
5 tablespoons mayonnaise
3 teaspoons minced onion
2 teaspoons prepared
   horseradish

1 teaspoon minced parsley
¼ teaspoon garlic salt
Paprika

Blend cheese and mayonnaise together in mixing bowl. Add onion, horseradish, parsley, and garlic salt. Blend well. Turn out into serving dish and dust with paprika. *Makes about 1 cup*

HE-MAN DIP

1 jar (5 ounces) sharp
   processed cheese spread
1 package (3 ounces)
   cream cheese, softened
⅓ cup catsup or chili sauce
⅓ cup finely chopped onion
2 tablespoons sweet pickle
   relish, drained

1 teaspoon prepared mustard
¼ teaspoon liquid smoke
6 slices bacon, fried crisp,
   crumbled
French fries

Blend all ingredients, except bacon and french fries, together in mixing bowl. Blend well. Stir in bacon. Serve with crisp french fries. *Makes 1¾ cups*

CHEESE-CHIVE DIP

1 package (8 ounces)
cream cheese, softened
⅓ cup mayonnaise
1 teaspoon Worcestershire
sauce

1 teaspoon minced chives
1 teaspoon seasoned salt
½ pound sharp American
cheese, shredded
French fries

Blend first 5 ingredients together in mixing bowl. Mix well until smooth and fluffy. Add American cheese and mix well. Serve with crisp french fries. *Makes 2½ cups*

TURMERIC ONION DIP

1 package (3 ounces)
cream cheese, softened
½ cup dairy sour cream
2 teaspoons instant minced
onion

¼ teaspoon salt
1⁄16 teaspoon garlic powder
½ teaspoon ground turmeric

Combine all ingredients in mixing bowl. Blend well. Turn out into serving dish and chill until ready to use. *Makes ¾ cup*

CARAWAY SEED DIP

1 package (8 ounces)
cream cheese, softened
4 tablespoons butter or
margarine
1¼ teaspoons salt
2 tablespoons paprika

1 teaspoon powdered dry
mustard
4 teaspoons whole caraway
seed
Crackers, potato chips, or
vegetable sticks

Combine cream cheese, butter, salt, paprika, mustard, and caraway seed in mixing bowl. Mix until all ingredients are blended. Chill. Remove from refrigerator about 1 hour before serving. Serve as a dip with crackers, potato chips, or vegetable sticks. *Makes 1¼ cups*

PINK PIMIENTO DIP

1 can (7 ounces) pimientos,
drained
2 tablespoons grated onion
1 tablespoon grated lemon
rind

1 package (8 ounces)
cream cheese, softened
½ teaspoon salt
¼ teaspoon pepper
½ to ¾ cup mayonnaise

Mash pimientos with onion, lemon rind, cream cheese, salt, and pepper in mixing bowl. Blend until smooth and creamy. Add mayonnaise and blend until mixture mounds easily. *Makes 2 cups*

PIMIENTO AVOCADO DIP

1 can (4 ounces) pimientos, finely chopped
1 cup mashed avocado
1 package (8 ounces) cream cheese, softened
1½ ounces Danish blue cheese, softened

3 tablespoons lemon juice
2 teaspoons horseradish
1 teaspoon salt
Dairy sour cream

Add pimiento and avocado to softened cheeses in mixing bowl. Blend until smooth. Mix in remaining ingredients with enough sour cream to make mixture mound easily. *Makes 1¾ cups*

DIP LATINA

1 medium-sized avocado
⅛ teaspoon salt
⅛ teaspoon onion powder
Dash cayenne

2 teaspoons lemon juice
¼ teaspoon Tabasco
¼ cup dairy sour cream

Cut avocado in half. Remove seed. Mash pulp. Combine avocado in mixing bowl with remaining ingredients. Cover immediately with protective wrap to prevent discoloration and chill until ready to use. *Makes ¾ cup*

AVOCADO DUNK

2 ripe avocados
½ cup mayonnaise
3 tablespoons lemon juice
1 teaspoon chili powder
1 small garlic clove, pressed,
   if desired

¼ teaspoon Tabasco
¼ teaspoon salt
Raw vegetables

Mash avocados with fork or place in blender and process until smooth. Stir in mayonnaise, lemon juice, chili powder, garlic, Tabasco, and salt. Cover immediately with protective wrap to prevent discoloration. Refrigerate for about 1 hour before serving to let flavors blend. Serve with raw vegetable dunkers such as cauliflower buds, green pepper slices, carrot sticks, or cucumber sticks. *Makes 1½ cups*

SALSA DIP

3 tablespoons onion flakes
3 tablespoons water
1 tablespoon olive oil
2 cups chopped tomatoes
¼ cup tomato paste
½ cup water
2 tablespoons green pepper
   flakes
1 bay leaf

2 teaspoons sugar
½ teaspoon oregano leaves,
   crushed
¼ teaspoon crushed red
   pepper
1½ teaspoons chili powder
⅛ teaspoon instant garlic
   powder

Combine onion flakes and water in small mixing bowl and set aside for 10 minutes to soften. Heat oil in a 1½-quart saucepan. Add onion and cook over low heat 10 minutes or until golden. Stir in chopped tomatoes, tomato paste, water, pepper flakes, bay leaf, sugar, oregano, and crushed red pepper. Cover and cook 15 minutes over low heat until thickened. Stir in chili and garlic powder and simmer 5 minutes more. Remove from heat. Serve hot or cold. *Makes 1½ cups*

GARLIC-BEAN DIP

1 can (8 ounces) red kidney beans	½ teaspoon onion salt
2 slices bacon	½ teaspoon chili powder
½ teaspoon instant garlic powder	¼ teaspoon ground black pepper
	1 cup dairy sour cream

Drain and mash kidney beans. Cook bacon until crisp and drain on absorbent paper before crumbling. Add mashed beans to warm bacon fat. Stir until all fat is absorbed. Remove from heat and allow to cool. Stir seasonings into mashed bean mixture. Fold in sour cream and crumbled bacon. Blend well. *Makes 2½ cups*

PEANUT-CHEESE DIP

½ cup chopped green
 pepper
¼ cup chopped onion
1 garlic clove, chopped
1 tablespoon peanut oil
1 can (8 ounces) tomato
 sauce
¼ teaspoon oregano

¼ teaspoon basil
¼ teaspoon chili powder
¼ teaspoon salt
⅛ teaspoon pepper
¼ pound Cheddar cheese,
 grated
¼ cup peanut butter

Combine green pepper, onion, and garlic in peanut oil in top of double boiler and cook over low heat until tender but not brown. Add tomato sauce, oregano, basil, chili powder, salt, and pepper. Cover and cook 10 minutes more, stirring occasionally. Add grated cheese and peanut butter. Assemble double boiler and cook over boiling water until cheese is melted and mixture is completely blended. Serve warm. *Makes 2 cups*

SWEET 'N' SOUR DIP

2 cups dairy sour cream
½ cup chopped cashews
2 tablespoons pickle relish

2 teaspoons grated onion
⅛ teaspoon Tabasco
Potato chips or crackers

Combine sour cream, cashews, pickle relish, grated onion, and Tabasco in mixing bowl. Blend well and chill until ready to use. Serve with potato chips or crackers. *Makes 2½ cups*

INDEX

Native New Yorker **William I. Kaufman** spends a large part of every year traveling to all areas of the world, gathering new and unusual recipes for his huge, famous collection. Out of his travels have come, literally, dozens of books on food and cooking. Among the popular cookbooks he has authored or co-authored, are: THE ART OF CREOLE COOKERY • THE 'I LOVE PEANUT BUTTER' COOKBOOK • THE COFFEE COOKBOOK • THE NUT COOKBOOK • THE HOT DOG COOKBOOK • THE ART OF INDIA'S COOKERY • THE TEA COOKBOOK • THE ART OF CASSEROLE COOKERY • THE APPLE COOKBOOK • THE 'I LOVE GARLIC' COOKBOOK • THE COTTAGE CHEESE COOKBOOK • THE FISH AND SHELLFISH COOKBOOK.